DATE DUE		

E L E P H A N T O M S

ELEPHANTOMS

TRACKING THE ELEPHANT

LYALL WATSON

W · W · NORTON & COMPANY

NEW YORK   LONDON

For information about permission to reproduce selections from this book, write to
Permissions, W. W. Norton & Company, Inc., 500 Fifth Avenue, New York, NY 10110

The text and display of this book are composed in Bodoni
Composition by Gina Webster
Manufacturing by Courier Westford
Book design and drawings by Margaret M. Wagner
Production manager: Julia Druskin

Library of Congress Cataloging-in-Publication Data
Watson, Lyall.
Elephantoms : tracking the elephant / Lyall watson. — 1st ed.
p. cm.
ISBN 0-393-05117-X (hardcover)
1. Elephants—History. I. Title.
QL737.P98 W375 2002
599.67—dc21   2002000318

W. W. Norton & Company, Inc., 500 Fifth Avenue, New York, N.Y. 10110
www.wwnorton.com

W. W. Norton & Company Ltd., Castle House, 75/76 Wells Street, London W1T 3QT

1 2 3 4 5 6 7 8 9 0

The idea of the elephant is imperishable.

ARTHUR SCHOPENHAUER

1833

CONTENTS

The
Stone
Age

LUKIE is seven, an alert and inquisitive child with all the innocent charm of those affected by Down's syndrome.

He doesn't talk much, but communicates well, conveying his needs and concerns through an extensive range of sounds and gestures.

His greatest pleasure is to walk with his father in the swamp forests around their home in central Florida. Lukie recognizes a wide range of animals there, identifying each with a sign of his own devising.

His father has become familiar with the code and confirms every sighting out loud as "wood stork," "garter snake," or "fox squirrel." They get along famously, but recently Lukie has begun to point out creatures his father can't see, and to describe these with a new and unfamiliar gesture.

This doesn't happen every day, but always follows a pause during which Lukie stops to listen to sounds his father can't hear. And sometimes he lifts one arm high over his head in a graceful arc and turns to point into the trees, making a soft sound which turns to a sigh of exasperation when his father clearly fails to understand.

It never helps to pretend to share in Lukie's experience. He won't fall for that, but the mystery was finally resolved during a television program which sent Lukie rushing about in high excitement, making the strange sign again and again. The family was watching a National Geographic Special called *Elephants: Out of Time, Out of Space!*

Armed with this insight, Lukie's father began to pay closer attention to the pattern of his son's enthusiastic observations.

There are, of course, no elephants running wild on the banks of the Withlacoochee River in Citrus County, but there were. Lots of them. Several species of proboscid once roamed these coral plains in the company of Paleo-Indian hunter-gatherers. In nearby Silver Springs, a complete mastodon skeleton was recovered recently, riddled with man-made projectile points!

Lukie's elephant sightings are sprinkled around his home, but concentrate largely on an ancient sinkhole at the eastern end of placid Lake Consuelo—"the Waters of Consolation." Sandhill cranes gather here still on the edge of an aquifer which feeds a permanent pond. This persists through the usual dry season, surviving the lowest water levels in living memory, and would probably have been a dependable waterhole even during far drier Pleistocene and postglacial times. Exactly the sort of place where thirsty elephants would have congregated!

Perhaps they still do, bridging a gap of ten thousand years, imbuing that particular glade with a persistent sort of elephantness that is apparent somehow to Lukie's special senses. And in this, maybe, he is not alone. . . .

CHAPTER ONE

Seeing the Elephant

To see the elephant. (U.S. slang):
to get experience of life,
to gain knowledge of the world.
—*Oxford English Dictionary*

AFRICA is the stable heart of old Gondwana, left exposed when other less constant continents drifted away 130 million years ago.

Today it straddles the equator, a vast plateau of ancient rock rising steeply from a narrow coastal strip that remains almost unbroken. There are very few inlets, bays, or gulfs on a coastline shorter than that of Europe.

In the south, a semicircle of misty cliffs plunges vertically eight hundred feet down into deep water that rises silently and suddenly at the rocks, sweeping the unwary away in a relentless undertow.

This is the Cape. The Cape of Storms, washed from the east by the warm flood of the Agulhas Current, bringing coral fish down to the edge of the Roaring Forties; and from the west by an enormous cold current—the Antarctic Drift—carrying penguins and fur seals up into the tropics.

There is no other country whose coasts face so great a stretch of completely open water. And none which divides two great seas of such different character, blurring the boundary between Atlantic and Indian Oceans, creating a unique climatic zone with its own idiosyncratic weather and its own peculiar flora, both of which have played a vital part in animal and human evolution.

THE Cape Floral Kingdom, one of just six major floral divisions in the world, is known as *fynbos* ("fine bush" in Afrikaans) and consists of more than 8,500 species, over 70 percent of which are found nowhere else on earth. It is a rough-edged, hard-leafed evergreen community of heaths, sedges, reedlike restios, delicate gladioli, proteas, aromatic citruses, and pelargoniums—all crowded into a rich palette of saturated colors that can involve as many as 120 different kinds of plants in an area the size of a billiard table.

The composition varies wildly from one slope to another, forging delicate partnerships and stretching out for six hundred miles along the coastal plain between the ocean and a range of mountains guarding the interior. These run roughly parallel to the shore and are older even than the geological disturbance which isolated Africa. They folded inward and upward 250 million years ago during the growing pains of Gondwana, crumpling as the great landmass adjusted to tectonic stress along a fault line that finally separated Africa from South America.

Ancient sedimentary deposits in the area stand now in disarray, some frozen in vertical throws ten thousand feet high, broken only by narrow *poorts* or gaps that allow inland rivers to escape to the sea. The seaward slopes are fresh, ragged, and beautiful, weathering from gray to gold and rose as the declining sun warms their peaks.

On the coastal plains at their feet, the rivers have cut deep

gorges, the mouths of which are mostly drowned by rising sea levels and then partly filled in by beds of marine fossils or chains of
lakes. All adding up to an exclusive ecosystem covering perhaps
thirty thousand square miles of rolling ground beneath the steep
walls of the Langeberg range, which run out eastward until they fall
into the sea.

All this happened long before there were elephants.

Proboscidean evolution began here in Africa roughly sixty million years ago, probably with a small creature about the size of a pig,
which wallowed in swampy depressions along the Valley of the Nile.
It has been called *Moeritherium*—"Beast from Lake Moeris"—and
had two elongated teeth projecting from each jaw and heavy lips
drawn out into a rudimentary trunk.

The eyes and ears of this animal were small and set high on the
head, as befits an amphibious lifestyle, but its most interesting feature was that its protruding teeth were not canines, but incisors—just
like the tusks of modern elephants. And like them it probably spent
a great deal of its time snorting and splashing in the shallows.

Moeritherium, or something very like it, seems to have evolved
directly into those unlikely sirens the modern sea cows and
dugongs, nearest living relatives of the elephants. But it also gave
rise to another line of development, one far more inventive,
concentrating on leaving the water and growing large as quickly
as possible.

BY the end of the Eocene, forty million years ago, all of dry land
Africa was dominated by two kinds of large plant-eating mammals:
the horse family, who grazed on a wide range of grassy plants; and
the antelope family, who browsed on the softer parts of more leafy
species. The only real gap in this terrestrial ecology was for a herbi-

vore able to take advantage of what was left of the woodier parts of trees and shrubs, which only a large animal with different adaptations could eat and digest.

The result was a riot involving over 350 aspiring species. Throughout the whole of the Miocene—a high point in mammalian evolution which ran from 26 to 6 million years ago—a splendid cast of experimental elephants appeared on the scene.

The first of these were over six feet tall with pillarlike legs and thick, heavy bones. They are known, collectively, as gomphotheres— a delightful name that translates literally as "beasts that are bolted together." It is an apt description for a range of prototypes such as the "four-tusker" *Tetrabeladon*; the bizarre "shovel-tusker" *Platybeladon*, which scooped up water plants with broad-bladed lower teeth; and the "straight-tusker" *Anancus*, which somehow managed to get across most of Africa with unwieldy tusks almost as long as its entire body.

ALL of these oddities were too specialized to last. They were evolutionary dead ends and doomed to disappear along with that bold innovation the deinothere—a "terrible beast" which departed from the mainstream by growing huge curved fangs in its lower jaw.

In all fairness, this large proboscid, which stood more than eight feet tall at the shoulder, did last for fifteen million years, and was finally found wanting only in the purely mechanical department. Its vampirelike lower jaw didn't work very well. A third-order lever with its fulcrum at the back of the lower jaw is much less efficient than the first-order levers used by more modern elephants, whose skull and tusks pivot on the center of the upper jaw.

Deinotherium and most of the early gomphotheres are routinely illustrated with trunks of various sizes, but such soft parts don't fossilize and it is more likely that the trunk really only developed into an organ in its own right once the lower jaw had shrunk and produced a far flatter face.

Modern elephants are all chinless wonders.

THE first true elephants appear only in the last six million years—in the Pliocene Period—beginning with *Primelephas*.

This, in retrospect, looks like a very canny candidate. It seems to have lurked in the African gene pool, hanging on to a number of primitive features such as having small tusks in both jaws, waiting for the more extravagant entrants in the evolutionary stakes to burn out and disappear.

We know very little about *Primelephas*, but it is generally agreed to represent the genetic source for all three modern genera of elephants.

One is *Loxodonta*, the African elephant; the second is *Elephas*, the Asian elephant; and the third was *Mammuthus*, a group of hairy elephants or mammoths that survived until the very end of the last Ice Age, getting frozen in Alaska and Siberia and being immortalized in numerous cave paintings.

It is significant that all three lines lived together with our immediate ancestors in only one place—in Africa. And it is of particular interest that such coincidence was common in the Cape.

PLACE names in South Africa abound. As the Boers (the early Dutch settlers) spread out into the interior, they called this alien world into more reassuring being by giving each new feature a name. Their own name. One drawn from a limited vocabulary that necessarily repeated itself again and again. So there are many Bloemfonteins (flowering springs), Uitzichts (lookouts), Grootdraais (big bends), Perdekops (horse's heads), and Rietvleis (reed ponds). Buffalos, lions, and crocodiles also feature prominently in this pioneering gazetteer, but by far the most common and evocative associations have to do with elephants.

There are literally hundreds of places called Olifantsrivier, Olifantsvlei, Olifantsfontein, Olifantsberg, or Olifantskop; but the one thing all these elephantine connections have in common is that there are no longer any elephants there. It is estimated that by the turn of the nineteenth century, there were only a few hundred wild elephants left anywhere in South Africa, nearly all of these in special reserves.

I was born in the north on one "River of the Elephants" and loved the name, but looked in vain for any eponymous beings. They had all long since disappeared—hunted, harried, or fenced out of existence. But something strong and strange remained. I never found a footprint or even a bleached bone on that riverfront, but I also never walked its banks alone.

There were great, gray ghosts everywhere. . . .

The same was true of the Cape Coast.

Liberated from boarding school, I spent my long summer holidays there, on the bay where the first European occupation of southern Africa took place. Bartholomeu Dias and Vasco da Gama had already rounded the Cape at the end of the fifteenth century, but they were hell-bent on getting to the Orient and had little time for Africa. Dias dismissed it with the words "There is no profit to be obtained from this land, so I will not waste time in describing it further."

Almost a century later, in 1576, Manuel da Mesquita da Perestrello, a less obsessed Portuguese trader, took the time to explore the coast more carefully and to anchor in one of the few protected bays. He called it Bahia Formosa ("Beautiful Bay") and marked it so conspicuously on the charts that in 1630 the *San Gonzales*, storm-damaged on its way back from the Spice Islands, took refuge in the same bay. A hundred men managed to get themselves and some supplies ashore before the vessel sank.

We know from a diary kept by the ship's priest, Friar Francisco Dos, that the castaways erected shelters and a church, planted gardens, hunted antelope and birds—and saw elephants on several occasions! The good friar made much of these encounters, but elephants were not totally unknown to Europe. Louis IX brought an African elephant back to France in the thirteenth century and sent it to his English brother-in-law Henry III, who housed it in the Tower of London.

In 1515, King Manuel I of Portugal offered an elephant as a gift to the Medici Pope Leo X, who provided it with magnificent accommodation in the Vatican gardens, where it was drawn by Raphael. Throughout the sixteenth and seventeenth centuries, elephants from North Africa continued to be valued gifts of state, flattering the recipients at the same time as they drew attention to the global grasp of the donors. But these elephants in Formosa Bay were probably the first wild ones ever seen by Europeans in southern Africa.

Eight months after the loss of their ship, the crew of the *San Gonzales* completed the building of two small open boats. They put half the crew in each and sent one boat east and the other west in search of aid. Despite incredible hardships, the friar and his crew managed to reach a Portuguese trading post a thousand miles away in Mozambique. The westbound boat was initially far more fortunate and was picked up just a few days into its journey by the trader *Loyola*, homeward bound for Portugal. But that ship, with all her crew and the castaways, was lost in a storm at the mouth of the Tagus, within sight of Lisbon!

*A*S children, we cherished these stories and searched through the dunes along Formosa Bay (now named Plettenberg Bay after a later Dutch governor) for any traces of the castaways. After three centuries, we found none, but were enthralled one year when the oak ribs of a wreck emerged from the beach after a severe storm, and had little hesitation in identifying it as the ill-fated *San Gonzales.*

It might have been, but there was a lot more substantial history at hand in the form of the ruins of a timber store and what was left of the Old Rectory, a Dutch gabled home with whitewashed walls three feet thick still standing just yards from the beach. Our family had the use of this abandoned building every Christmas and overflowed in our camp beds out onto a wide verandah, where we fell asleep each night to thoughts of elephants wandering still in single file down to the shores of old Formosa Bay, and to the quavering sound of fiery-necked nightjars locked in litany, chanting their six-note response: "Good Lord, deliver us; Good Lord, deliver us; Good Lord, deliver us."

He did. It was a golden age. We rose each day before dawn to go fishing from the Lookout Rocks, casting fresh fillets of a small orange-striped bream out, unweighted, just beyond the breakers, reeling these slowly back in ways carefully designed to tempt passing shad. Shoals of these predatory fish, known locally as *elf,* cruised the coast each summer, feeding at dawn and dusk, snatching at the right bait, putting up an exhilarating fight, snapping at careless fingers with small, razor-sharp teeth. Their flesh was firm and white and spoiled quickly, softening within the hour, but taken directly and triumphantly back to the Rectory and grilled whole on an open spit . . . there was no better breakfast!

The days were spent beach-walking, swimming, body-surfing, growing blond and brown. We were too old for Christmas and too young for girls, but never felt the lack of either or knew a moment's boredom. The six weeks of summer went by all too quickly, and the only consolation that came with returning to school each January was the knowledge that we were one year nearer graduation—not from school, but from being under ten and therefore not allowed to join the Strandlopers!

WHEN the Dutch landed at the Cape in 1652 to establish the first formal settlement, they were approached almost immediately by a small group of people.

This welcoming committee consisted of men, women, and children, all small and tawny-colored, with hair curled into peppercorns. They wore brief loincloths, pointed skin caps, and leather capes—the *kaross*—draped over their shoulders. Some had leggings of rawhide strips wrapped around their ankles, and all carried a stick or shoulder bag.

They lived right there on the beaches, collecting shellfish, crayfish, or birds' eggs and dining, when they could, on fur seal and the occasional beached whale. The colonists called them *strandlopers* ("beachwalkers") and judged, from the huge midden mounds of mussel and oyster shell, that they had lived in this way for a very long time.

Such mounds still exist. Their fragments of shell shine like beacons, visible even at a distance all along the old raised beaches, now fifty feet or more above the present high-tide line. We were curious about these accumulations and, from time to time on slow days, dug into them, finding shells shaped to provide a sharp cutting edge, or pieces of bird bone ground to a fine point like an awl.

The Dutch were rather dismissive of these "savages" who scavenged for food, ate it raw, and slept on the sand. But we liked what we heard, admired their ingenuity, and were very taken by their lifestyle and their given name. Beach-walking, in our eyes, was an entirely reasonable and honourable profession.

"*WE*" in all these matters is not a grand royal pronoun, but a first person plural that describes an informal tribal gathering of boys belonging to several families whose only common cause was that they spent their summer holidays on the coast near Plettenberg Bay.

This all took place more than half a century ago, but our lemminglike migration to the sea each year had already been going on long enough by then to have acquired its own traditions. The most venerable of these were centered on a fishing camp, actually just a one-room hut in the dunes, constructed entirely from driftwood accumulated over the course of several generations.

This ramshackle hideaway lay along the coast on the land of a friendly farmer whose great-grandfather had enjoyed the company of our great-grandfathers, who gathered there whenever they could to enjoy an all-male *braaivleis* (barbecue), some good brandy, and some truly great lies about all the fish they had caught.

Children were not normally included in these gatherings, but in the mid-twentieth century our fathers were either away fighting a world war or struggling to rebuild professions or businesses disrupted by that war, and could not afford to take long vacations. They stayed on in the cities and joined their women and children only over Christmas and the New Year.

This worked reasonably well, but didn't allow for the postwar coincidence that almost all the children of our generation were boys, who ran a little wild without paternal supervision. Being bad in those innocent days wasn't a big deal—cadging the occasional cigarette or borrowing someone's bicycle without permission. The odd urge to rebel was easily and harmlessly satisfied, but nevertheless disturbing to mothers who were hoping to enjoy their own break from routine domesticity.

Their solution was brilliant. They talked the farmer into allowing some of the boys, the most unruly ones, to spend time camping out in the hut on their own. And as the hut lay miles from the farmhouse and contained nothing of any value, he readily agreed.

So the hut became a clubhouse and something more, something impossible in these dangerous days, a place where a dozen young boys were allowed to live for an entire month without adult supervision. And as any half-decent club has to have members and a proper name—we became the Strandlopers.

THE Club Rules were simple:

1. No girls allowed.
2. No boys under ten or over thirteen could belong.
3. Everyone shared everything.
4. Nobody left before the month was out.

The first Beachwalkers were breaking new ground and had a lot of help. They were taken out to the hut in wagons and provided with enough canned food, water, and creature comforts to last the month. In those early days, mothers who panicked were allowed one maternal visit bearing food packages and Christmas gifts, but as it turned out they were not welcome. The boys managed very well, and each year the supplies and the conditions became more Spartan.

Living on the shore, sleeping on the floor, catching and collecting most of what they needed, the new Strandlopers took a fierce pride in their ability to support themselves. And before long it became mandatory to take in only what the group themselves could carry in on foot. Which meant nothing more than flour, sugar, soap, candles, matches, fishing gear, a first-aid kit, and one change of clothes. No visitors were allowed, but it was understood that in an emergency, three of the tribe would make the walk to the nearest telephone at the farm.

The span of ages at the club meant that there was always continuity. As each group of ten-year-old recruits joined the band, they were taught survival skills by the outgoing thirteen-year-old members, and so a continuous culture was born, or at least reinvented. And all the contributing families noticed the same thing. Even their most awkward offspring returned from the hut with a new maturity, with a different bearing, with what one of the fathers, who had seen the same thing in the faces of men returning from a difficult military mission, described as "the far look."

I have seen that look since, on the faces of villagers in Indonesia who make their living hunting whales in open boats. They wear it well when taking excess meat to market to exchange with farmers in the hills. It defines the difference between hunting and cultivating, between the Stone Age and the Iron Age, between chivalry and husbandry. Part of it is a simple pride in being able to look after yourself, but there is also the sort of satisfaction that can only come from living dangerously and getting away with it.

What we younger ones noticed most was that the returning Strandlopers were uncharacteristically tight-lipped. All they would say was: "Wait until you turn ten."

Waiting is hell, but no amount of cajoling made any difference, and we were forced to hang on for several very long years, making the best use we could of snippets that leaked out about the great adventure. We knew it must be great, because nobody, not one boy in the whole known history of the club, ever failed to spend all of his four allotted summers at the hut.

I certainly did. Those four months remain among the best ones of my life. And one month, in particular, still governs much of what I feel and do.

Each summer began in the same way. We were dropped off at the farmhouse with our gear and trudged through soft sand and scrub for hours. There was not much to see but an ostrich or two and small groups of springbok, which on scenting us *pronked* away, raising a crest of snow-white hair on their rumps as they leapt six feet or more into the air, paddling with their hind legs in a dramatic display of high spirits and tight sinews, alerting other antelope to the presence of potential danger.

It was always hot on the plain, but everything changed as we neared the coast and could smell the sea. The scrub was replaced by the maritime forest that tumbled over the cliffs and down ravines in a thick olive-green cover of salt-tolerant trees with gnarled trunks and small shiny leaves. There were several dominant species, all old and slow-growing and each fragrant in a way that combined into an unforgettable, spicy smell that is peculiar to the Cape. Just one whiff of it still carries me right back to those halcyon days, and I can hear the sound of the surf and see small, glittering gold-and-blue butter-flies in the air.

There was a path through the forest, kept open by bushbuck and bushpig, which led all the way down to Sandy Bay, a narrow beach with a submerged reef providing sheltered water at one end and a promontory at the other, known to fishermen as Roman Rock. Nothing Italianate, this outcrop owed its name to a deep drop-off famous for its red romans—fish of the bream family that are scar-let-orange in color and come up from the depths at the end of a line like a flame burning underwater.

Just above this, on the edge of a dune and beneath an old and shady milkwood tree, was the equally famous hut. There wasn't a single right angle in its construction and it leaned amiably in sev-eral directions, but timber of a dozen different kinds, all bleached by salt and sun to the same well-used pale gray, gave it a surprising dignity. Inside there was nothing but a wooden floor with gaps between the planks large enough to provide ventilation and to let beach sand trickle back through, and walls festooned with pegs and a small selection of pots and pans.

I liked it right away.

FORAGING feels good. Blaise Pascal was right, our true nature does lie in movement, and if such restlessness also provides food, all the better.

There is a huge difference between foraging for fun and doing so because you are hungry. So as soon as it was light on that first morning, we novice Strandlopers began our apprenticeship with lessons in self-sufficiency. The tide was going out, and Petrus—a Grade Two Strandloper, better known to us as the Rock—showed us how to find lunch.

Every high tide leaves a line of foam and flotsam on the beach. Most of this is vegetable matter, but there are always bits of transparent jelly or remnants of the pale blue floats of Portuguese men-of-war. These were occasional hazards we learned to avoid, but they did bring out the blind scavenging whelks, who feed only at night and bury themselves at first light. They are the world's fastest-burrowing snails, disappearing in less than a second, but on a falling tide they leave telltale tracks.

The Rock was born to fish. He was the youngest of a famous family of great fishermen. His parents wanted him, like his brothers, to go on to university and make something better of his life, but the Rock loved the intertidal zone and foraging for himself. And, unlike them, he did not simply dismiss anything without scales as "bait."

"Look for furrowed tracks," he suggested, "like a tiny plow just passed this way. They go every which way on wet sand, but if you look carefully you can see where the muscular footmark is, and where this is obscured by the shell that drags behind it. Follow that and where it ends, dig down about a hand's depth—and do it quickly!"

He did and came up with a pale, smooth, spiral shell attached to a white muscle that wriggled and squirted water at him.

"Soup," he said, smacking his lips. And within ten minutes we had hats full of enough whelks to make a meal to go with unleavened bread baked in a biscuit-tin oven.

The best thing about well-informed foraging is that it doesn't take long, leaving lots of time for other activities. We spent the rest of the morning swimming and didn't think about food again until the early afternoon. That was dedicated to cast-netting on an incoming tide, and once again the Rock showed the way.

He took the net line in his teeth, draping the body of net over one arm as he began to gather up the rest of the weighted edge in his other hand. "Like feeling your way under a girl's skirt," he explained.

We ten-year-olds squirmed in disgust, but never forgot the useful image, and after a number of practice casts, managed to ensnare a three-pound *galjoen* in the surf.

This is one of the Cape's unique species and almost South Africa's national fish. It comes close inshore at high tide, turning in a breaking wave, with scales tough enough to protect it from contact with the rocks. It feeds on black mussels, which abound in shallow water, and explodes into frantic action in a net or at the end of a line.

The flesh has a rather strong, salty flavor, but once it is allowed to bleed out and has been completely scaled, it tastes wonderful grilled in slow-burning coals on the beach.

Being a Strandloper was fine!

EACH summer the mix was a little different. There were three or four boys from each age group, but only the youngest in their first season in the club were identifiable as a separate class. They were new boys, having to learn the ropes, being thrown together more often than not, while the rest of us were old hands.

But we were all Strandlopers and proud of it, well aware that these summers set us apart from other boys who got fed, driven about, and told what to do. We were a different tribe, a democracy while it lasted and happy to make things up as we went along. Our society was never large enough to splinter into factions or small enough to come to blows, but by accident something very close to the optimal group size for all successful foragers and hunter-gatherers throughout history.

The distinctions that did emerge amongst us were all based on merit and ability. We deferred to the Rock on anything to do with fishing. He seemed always to know when and where to go and what kind of catch to expect. Boetie, a tough Afrikaner kid who grew up on a farm in Pondoland where he kept company with local herd boys, automatically took charge of setting snares and deadfall traps for rabbits and guinea fowl. What he caught he also cooked, doing a delicious fowl baked in its own juices by burying it in a cocoon of clay beneath our evening fire. And Julius—better known as Owl because of his thick, round glasses—was accepted, by acclaim, as court jester. He filled every gap in any circumstance with an appropriate aside or well-timed pratfall that left us all in tears.

I found myself, from the second year on, acting as the equivalent of tribal shaman. It was largely a matter of knowledge. I had taught myself to read long before I went to school, devouring every piece of print that came to hand. At least a book a day. And I had the huge advantage, during the early years of the World War, of being raised largely by a Zulu mentor who was a healer and diviner, what was then known as a "witch doctor."

So I got called "Doc" Watson and slid easily into the role of storyteller, mythmaker, and keeper of old and newly minted tradition for the Strandlopers. It was my job, when disagreements did arise, to arbitrate by dredging up historical or purely fictional authority which absolved us all, individually, from having to take sides.

"That is how it was done" ruled the day and most of our after-dinner discussions—and still leaves me with huge respect for the power of precedent and tradition.

But the biggest lesson we all learned was that of free association. There was just enough that needed to be done each day to keep us fed, watered, warm, and secure, to give every one of us a role to play. Whether it was finding food, hauling water, collecting firewood, or keeping watch, each of us, every day, did something useful without finding it a chore. There were never lists or allotted tasks, no arguments about who did or didn't do something. Everything, every year, just got done because we were all Strandlopers, doing what was necessary to keep us out there where we wanted to be.

Liberty, we discovered, was the essential prerequisite. Equality, fraternity, and all the rest of those good things seem to follow naturally on.

Looking back, I am amazed by how well it all worked. Young boys are better known for rebellion than collaboration, but in hindsight I am also aware of a factor that pushed us in the right direction. Life on that beach was easy. There was always something to eat, something different almost every day. The climate was kind, we lived in swimsuits supplemented by a shirt or sweater in the evenings, and we all felt so comfortable there. As though we fitted into a gap in the ecology, a niche ready waiting for us to arrive.

That magic feeling, that sense of the appropriate, is an important part of the Cape experience. It is precisely what has made this place so special, so seminal to the history and development of so many unique species.

THERE were problems, of course.

We had to find our own fresh water. One of the early groups had rolled a large drum down to the site and set this up to catch rain-water from the tin roof of the hut. But, unlike the rest of Africa, the Cape Coast is a winter rainfall area and gets little further moisture during the summer months. So we had to look for supplementary sources, and soon discovered that the best guides to these were the bushpig.

These are real wild pigs with shaggy coats and grizzled gray faces. They are cautious and largely nocturnal, and they travel in family groups that always include a trotterful of spotted piglets. They eat almost anything, but must have water and are very skillful at finding it. There were seasonal springs on the cliffs, and down at the beachfront, where rock met sand, good water accumulated just beneath the surface. All you had to do was to look for signs of recent digging, scrape sand carefully out of a hollow there until it turns damp, and then wait for it to fill with a trickle of cool, delicious, finely filtered water.

And when even the pigs failed, we discovered that we could drink the early-morning mists by going out to one of the steep ravines, pushing our faces deep into the carpets of absorbent moss that grew there—and sucking!

It was fine foraging for food, but wringing water out of the rocks or dunes was rewarding in an entirely different way. There was something more spiritual about that. Something which resonates in us, which not just satisfies thirst, but also soothes the soul. Making sense of the reflex which sends us rushing for glasses of water for victims of shock, injury, or sheer stage fright, and leads in dry climates to ritual offerings of water as part of a welcome ceremony.

You can push your chair back from the dining table with a word of thanks or a grunt of gratification and a summary demand for the bill. But a draft of cool, clear water requires a different response, something softer, more gracious, much more like benediction. Water is a gift, and being asked to pay for it amounts almost to blasphemy.

Bottled water with a designer label is something else altogether. Just another commodity.

FREE water is impressionable. Its chemistry is simple, just two atoms of hydrogen and one of oxygen, but no molecule of it exists in isolation. For water to occur at all, it has to be intricately interlaced. It is, in truth, held together by so many hydrogen bonds that it is an almost continuous structure. Even a lake is, in effect, one giant molecule with all its parts interconnected. And this gives water, wherever it may be, both extraordinary strength and astonishing flexibility.

Just like elephant society. No elephant can exist alone for long. It is part of a larger whole, a network so diffuse that an extended herd can cover hundreds of square miles. A "web" of sound connects each part, turning their apparently thin scatter into one great thick-skinned organism. One with enviable integrity and a surprising sensitivity.

Elephants and water go together. They have an amazing affinity. In arid areas, only elephants can find and reach subterranean sources and make them available to other thirsty species. They seem to have an elementary knowledge of geology, digging most often in likely places close to the entrance of tributaries, or on the outer edge of wide curves in dry riverbeds where water once flowed most rapidly and deeply.

Sometimes, however, they choose to dig right out in the open, a mile from anywhere in a sandy waste, and still succeed.

Can they smell water percolating through the soil several feet underground? Possibly. Or is some other sense responsible? A necessary precondition for resonance between things is that they should be compatible, having similar structures or compositions. Elephants are two-thirds water to start with, just as we are, but they have the advantage of greater volume and a pair of antennae or built-in divining rods in the form of their tusks. And it is also possible that they could be using a sonar system based on the echoes of their own footfalls!

When the wells they dig with toes and trunks are too deep for young calves to use, adults have been seen drawing up water in their trunks and pouring it into their infants' mouths. And in emergencies, all elephants have access to an as yet unexplained and undiscovered reservoir of water. One they suck up out of their own throats and spray onto ears and backs to help keep cool.

Life's dependence on water is total and very precise. Water absorbs heat reluctantly and, true to its contrary nature, unevenly. In most other substances, the amount of heat needed to increase temperature by 1°C is the same for each degree involved. But not with water. Between 35° and 40°C, water is unusually relaxed and most easily warmed. And this narrow range happens to coincide, if you still believe in such accidents, with the usual body temperature of both elephants and humans. Which is not only convenient, but may be crucial. It could even be the trigger that makes living things feel that water is so special, or that wells so often are considered to be holy.

A WIDER search for new sources of water in my third year in the club, a very dry year, led inadvertently to enlarged Strandloper horizons.

I was twelve, a senior member involved in patrolling beyond the immediate area of Sandy Bay. This usually meant just a gentle foray along the coast to the east as far as Rooikrans, where the cliffs turned a vivid rusty color, to see what might have washed up on the rocks below. Or a sortie to the west past Platbank, a flat rock in the water where cormorants dried their wings in the sun, and Losklip ("Loose Stone"), an unstable scree where it was easy to slip and fall.

We always went out in threes. One to go for help and one to stay with an injured member. Owl, who was my age, and I took a new boy with us that day. A quiet kid called Starbuck because we had discovered that he never said much, but when he did he was, like Captain Ahab's first mate, worth listening to.

Owl and Starbuck got on well. Owl did all the talking and Starbuck did all the listening. On that particular morning, the subject was elephants, because I had talked the previous evening about elephants and, in particular, about the wild elephants that still lived not far away in the Knysna forest—the southernmost elephants in the world and the only free-ranging elephants anywhere in southern Africa. And as we walked, I was explaining that this small herd once roamed over the whole coastal plain, taking advantage of grassland, fynbos, and swamp, but were now restricted to about a thousand square miles of high forest where the thick undergrowth made them very hard to see.

Owl couldn't resist it: "Why do elephants wear dark glasses?"
Silence.
"For camouflage!"
More silence.
"Have you ever seen an elephant with dark glasses?"
No response.
"No? Just shows how good it works!" Followed by long, triumphant, solo laughter.

Starbuck just rolled his eyes and kept on walking. We were making our way with care along the upper edge of loose stone at Losklip, heading for a deep gorge that marked the agreed edge of Strandloper country. At this point a river ran into the sea, dragging an arm of forest right down to where the waves broke.

Getting down there and back was a day's work, and we never bothered. Nobody did. It was completely untouched and the cliffs on the far side were almost vertical, home only to hyraxes—rabbit-sized little mammals much given to basking in the sun, blinking and trying to come to terms with the extraordinary fact that, according to the structure of their feet and teeth, they were closely related to elephants!

We stopped there to watch these *dassies*, and to admire the view and catch our breaths. All except Owl, who never seemed to need to do so.

"How do you stop an elephant from charging?"

I reached for my stick.

"Take away its credit card!" But before Owl could join in his own applause, there was a sharp hiss from Starbuck.

"Shuddup Owl."

We both looked at the kid with astonishment, but Starbuck's attention was elsewhere. He stood like a statue, frozen in midstep, mouth open, eyes wide and fixed on the top of the cliffs across the gorge. And when we followed his gaze, we too became riveted.

There was a giant milkwood tree, growing out on its own, an old one, its branches festooned with beards of lichen, well placed to intercept the sea mist. I knew the tree well, it was said to be over a thousand years old, but today it looked different. Standing in its shade was another giant, a great gray shape so large that at first glance the eye passed right over it, accepting it as just part of the landscape. But then something else registered in my brain, somewhere in my memory bank patterns were compared and found to coincide, throwing up a conclusion so unlikely that it forced its way into conscious attention.

We were looking at an elephant!

A FULLY grown African elephant, facing left, staring out to sea, his thick white tusks shining in the shade beneath a broad round brow. Hips high and sway-backed, his undersides sloping up toward long front legs, he stood there like a monument, coming into full reality only when an ear the size of a blanket billowed.

Elephants have an uncanny knack of just blending into a natural background, something they do so well perhaps because they follow its flow. No elephant is ever completely still. The tip of the trunk is in constant motion and waves of awareness ripple through the thick skin like wind on water as it shifts its great weight from one great shock-absorbing footpad to another.

We watched enthralled. He turned his great head slightly in our direction, as if to let us see him to his best advantage, and as he did so, both tusks came into view. They were enormous, bulging from their sockets on either side of his trunk, thick and smooth at the base, darkening slightly at the midpoint, then lightening on the tip he used for digging. The point of the left tusk was very gently curved inward, toward the other, almost meeting near the ground in a grace note of such elegant asymmetry that it served only to emphasize his perfection.

But that was not all. To start with, our eyes and minds were full of the elephant, taking in his size, his stance, the way he seemed to grow out of the cliff. He was magnificent and something more, something that made him almost unreal. Something about his color. . . .

With elephants, color is usually an indication of recent history. A red or burnt-ocher overlay is a sign of wallowing in mud pools out on the grasslands, where everything is tinged with the rusty dust of the savanna. Dirty gray indicates time spent on the riverbanks, where the soil is richer with the dark sediments of erosion upstream. Paler hues suggest a salt lick, a clay pit, or simply a long time between baths during a drought.

White elephants are rare. In Asia, rare enough to have immense symbolic significance. They tend to be partial albinos with pink or yellow eyes and white patches at the edge of the ears and the base of the trunk. Sometimes the entire skin surface has a creamy tinge, putting such animals almost beyond price in Burma or Thailand, where they still command the kind of reverence and attention which requires very deep pockets.

African albinos seldom live long. Their susceptibility to bright light and overheating puts them at a huge disadvantage on the savanna or desert margins. They may fare better in temperate or forested areas such as the Cape Coast. But the elephant we were looking at was not an albino. There was nothing washed-out or blotchy about him, none of the ghostly pallor that indicates a lack of pigment. On the contrary, he was clearly in robust good health, everything an elephant should be, except that he wasn't gray or dusty, but more like patinated bronze or the color of old ivory.

Time seemed to stand still as he held his imperial pose. Then, backing up gently, he made a graceful three-point turn and vanished without a puff of dust into the shadows of the forest behind him. One moment he was there, and the next he was gone—and we remembered how to breathe again.

"*WOW!*" said Starbuck quietly.

Owl was struck dumb, lost for once for words. I was shaking, overwhelmed by a strange combination of privilege and awe. I had seen elephants before and at closer quarters, but this sighting was different. This elephant was ours, unfenced, unexpected, unaware of us. We were not enclosed in a vehicle, he was not restrained by our presence across the gorge. It seemed he was there for a purpose. His calm demeanor was regal and something else, a hint of reverence perhaps, as though this was something he did from time to time, a kind of ritual, a way of communing, one monarch to another, with the sea.

I learned later that elephants are indeed drawn to the ocean. Joyce Poole, who has given her life to studying elephants in Kenya, tells of them sliding down steep dunes on the Northern Frontier to swim in the sea. And of six elephants that crossed a deepwater channel to get to the deserted island of Manda "to enjoy the view and to listen to the breakers crashing against the rocks below"—only to be gunned down during their devotions by poachers who had followed them there and do not recognize the concept of sanctuary.

In the Bay of Bengal, herds of elephants have been seen swimming for over six hours to cross the mighty mouth of the Ganges. And further south, starting presumably from the delta of the Irrawaddy, a small group of elephants have successfully navigated over two hundred miles of open ocean to live on, and in the clear blue waters between, the stepping-stones of the Andaman Islands.

Was this bull of ours contemplating such a migration? Or was he just enjoying the sea breeze?

Fifteen minutes later, it was hard to believe he had happened. We checked with each other to make sure we had indeed seen the same thing and felt the same excitement.

Starbuck put it best. He shook his head and said wonderingly: "I didn't know. . . ."

ONE doesn't.

If elephants didn't exist, you couldn't invent one. They belong to a small group of living things so unlikely they challenge credulity and common sense. Animals such as aardvarks, hammerhead sharks, and star-nosed moles. All so odd they can only be described in terms of something else, something more familiar.

There is nothing quite like an elephant. Nothing with which it can be compared, though the proverbial Six Blind Men of Indostan did their best, likening each part encountered separately to a snake, a spear, a fan, a wall, a tree, and a rope. Taken altogether, these ingredients add up to a most singular animal whose trunk alone is enough to justify removing the elephant from the rest of the animal kingdom and setting it aside, along with ourselves perhaps, in categories of our own.

And yet, when you see an elephant, as we just had, embedded in its own earth, comfortable in its own skin, carrying its great weight effortlessly along on cushioned feet, the only possible response is: "Of course. How could it be otherwise?"

Elephants exist, even if represented now by only two or three of their 353 known species. They would seem to be on their way out, but it is still possible to argue that they represent the most highly evolved form of life on the planet. Compared to them, we are primitive, hanging on to a stubborn, unspecialized five-fingered state, clever but destructive. They are models of refinement, nature's archangels, the oldest and largest land animals, touchstones to our imagination.

Elephants are symbols of might and memory, harmony and patience, power and compassion. We are equivocal about them, as we are about anything which evokes strong feelings in us. We love and fear them, kill and revere them, see them as "beasts of the moon with crescent tusks" or as buffoons in baggy pants.

In captivity, their enormousness is muted, cloaked in indignity and shame, a source of acute dismay. But in the wild, they invoke awe, exercising uncanny skills, taking obvious delight in one another as they shuffle through our lives, keeping grave appointments at the other end of the world.

There is much about them that remains mysterious.

THE elephant had gone, leaving the three of us looking at his stand-ins, the undeniably cute but inadequate hyraxes.

They too walk on calloused soles and have four toenails on their front feet and three on their hind ones. They share also in the possession of two tusklike teeth in their upper jaws, but there the resemblance ends. These "little brothers of the elephant" sprawled all over the rocks on the edge of the cliffs, trying very hard to look enigmatic, and failing hopelessly.

We turned away reluctantly and were about to start on our way back to the hut when something totally unexpected stopped us in our tracks again.

It was just a sound at first, high-pitched and birdlike. A cackle similar to the harsh sunrise call of a territorial red-necked francolin, but then it changed, slowly and surely, into something more breathy.

We whirled around, raising our hiking sticks in unison to meet the challenge, startled to be confronted out here on the coast where nobody else belonged. Where none of us can remember ever having been disturbed by another of our kind. And what we saw didn't help.

The sound came from a figure hunched in among the rocks. A small brown being with wrinkled skin and tiny hands clasped around his knees as he rocked forward and backward, crowing and keening, gasping for breath. Our first impression was of a goblin in agony, but as the sound went on, seeming to come from deep in his belly, growing louder each time he looked at our faces, it became obvious that he was not crying, but laughing. Laughing at us!

When the fit finally passed and he was able to stand, he proved to be shorter than any of us. He was dressed in a sheepskin cape, worn with the wool next to his skin, and a conical cap that leaned over at the top like the toe of a stocking. His feet were bare and thickly calloused and he carried a soft bag slung across his back. In his hands was a stick which he held across his body like a soldier presenting arms.

We kept our sticks at the ready, pointing at him like fixed bayonets, but were immediately disarmed by a warm, gap-toothed smile. He walked down our line, for all the world like a visiting dignitary taking inspection of an honor guard, looking at our eyes, our ears, our sunburned skin. After weeks on the beach wearing next to nothing, we were almost as dark as he was. But when Starbuck lifted his hat to mop his brow, our visitor got a look at his salt-bleached blond hair and started laughing all over again.

It was a wonderful, uninhibited laugh—one that racked his whole body and soon infected ours. Before long we were all giggling, and then laughing with him, for no apparent reason.

AS long ago as the fourth century B.C., Aristotle suggested that laughter had a corrective function. That comedy was a social adjustment, a way of reconciling contradictions and bringing misfits back into society. The twentieth-century French philosopher Henri Bergson went further, pointing out that laughs, which necessarily begin nervously, reflect the contradiction between civilized society and our animal nature. They certify the awkward by acknowledging it, even celebrating it, allowing the different and the dangerous to be incorporated safely into our lives.

William Hazlitt in his essay "On Wit and Humour" said, "Man is the only animal that laughs," but anyone who has studied animal behavior knows that is not true. If you tickle a chimpanzee (it would be wise to choose a young one to start with), it narrows its eyes, relaxes its facial muscles, opens the mouth without showing its teeth, and, pulling in its neck and rolling the head from side to side, makes a series of soft and breathy grunts. These sound like, and serve precisely the same function as, gentle laughter. This allows the chimp to release its own anxiety about such close contact, and to signal a lack of aggression. It functions like social cement, defusing a potentially difficult situation.

We laugh most easily in two circumstances. The obvious one is by license. By being involved in an occasion defined as comic where, along with others, we hope and expect to be amused. Under these circumstances, we are less likely to be offended or alarmed because, in England at least, humor makes allowances for the rude, the foolish, and the truly incongruous. The ineptitude and insensitivity of Basil Fawlty are not threatening onscreen. It is all a game.

The second circumstance involves situations which are novel enough to make us feel uneasy. Under these conditions, we laugh nervously, just like a chimp, in the hope of deflecting possible aggression. If this seems to be working, we laugh more confidently, with relief. And if that goes well, the chances are that everyone involved gets caught up in one of those peculiar laugh fests that are mindless, but wonderfully cathartic.

WE were. Owl and Starbuck and I laughed until our stomachs ached.

We liked this strange little guy, and as soon as we could pull ourselves together, we took a walk around him, making an inspection of our own. He held still for this, and the first thing we noticed was that he smelled familiar. I couldn't place it at first, but soon remembered that it came from a local plant called *buchu*, one of the citrus family with oily glands in the leaves that release a strong fruity fragrance. We learned later that he mixed it with animal fat and rubbed his whole body with it at regular intervals, partly because it felt good, keeping his skin supple in the sun, and partly because it repelled biting flies and masked his own odor while hunting.

I said *"Buchu"* out loud when the name came to me, and there was an instant response. He reacted with delight and an explosive vocal combination of pops, clicks, whip cracks, and lip smacks, as though a case of Coca-Cola had been caught in a bush fire.

And it was then that we realized who and what our visitor was. This was someone whose direct ancestors, perhaps twenty generations ago, welcomed the first settlers to these shores. One early account records: "Their usual greeting on meeting us is a song, of which the beginning, the middle and the end is *hautitot.*" So the Dutch called them "Hottentots." But their own name for themselves was Khoikhoi, which means "Men of Men," "Real Men."

This was a *real* Strandloper!

CHAPTER TWO

Hearing the Elephant

To use silence so well: if I could
choose for people one attribute
of elephants, I'd choose this.
—KATY PAYNE in *Silent Thunder*, 1998

PORTUGAL in the fifteenth century was restless. It had a long
ocean frontage, a narrow hinterland, and a ruler so outward-looking
they called him Henry the Navigator.

Henry set up a school for mariners overlooking the ocean at
Sagre, which became the Cape Canaveral of its day, sending expeditions out to colonize Madeira, the Azores, and the Cape Verde
Islands. Toward the end of the century they developed the caravel,
a modified fishing vessel with three masts and lateen sails. This was
light, fast, and so maneuverable it opened up a whole new world.
One of gold and ivory, spices and slaves.

In 1487, Bartholomeu Dias was ordered to find the southern tip
of Africa and set off with three vessels and a company including the
leading pilots of the day. They hugged the coast until early the following year, when storms forced them west and out of sight of land

for several days. When they were able to turn east again, no land appeared, and it was only by sailing back north they regained contact with the continent again on February 3, 1488. They had rounded the Cape of Storms without seeing it, and were in the Indian Ocean!

Dias landed to set up a *padrão*, a stone pillar carried by the Portuguese to stake out the claim of their crown, and his crew were helping themselves to fresh water from a convenient spring when they were pelted with stones from an overlooking hill. Dias replied with crossbows, killing one of the defenders of this precious watering place, and setting the scene for centuries of contention between Europeans and the inhabitants of the Cape.

FOR the next 165 years, visits were sporadic. All coastal people were lumped together as "blacks" and variously labeled "ugly," "shameless," and "treacherous." A reputation earned early in the sixteenth century when Francesco de Almeida, viceroy of Portuguese India, stopped off at the Cape, captured several children, stole a herd of cattle, and was "shamelessly" killed, along with a number of his men, by a local force of furious parents.

By the time that Jan van Riebeeck arrived in 1652 to create a post for supplying Dutch East India crews with fresh meat and vegetables, things had settled down somewhat. Sailors had discovered that the coastal people lacked metal and valued it highly enough to exchange an entire ox for just two knives, a whole sheep for a handful of iron nails.

WE latter-day Strandlopers were somewhat nonplussed by our tawny new friend. After the *buchu* breakthrough, he wouldn't stop talking. We understood as little of his language as the Dutch did three hundred years before, but at least we had a starting point, something in common: the extraordinary White Elephant.

When I was able to hold his attention, I pointed across the gorge to where we had seen the old bull. He nodded and smiled and squatted down on the pathway to sketch with his stick in the sand.

First a circle about twenty inches wide with four crescent-shaped scoops at one end. Then a separate oval, more narrow, with just three scallops and, at the other side, a distinct scuff mark. Both diagrams he filled with a mosaic pattern and then sat back satisfied, as well he might.

What he had done, with a few deft artistic strokes, was to recreate the tracks of an adult elephant, probably male by its size, complete with hoofprint, nails, and the characteristic toe-drag mark all elephants leave with their trailing hind feet.

We said: "Elephant!"

He smiled, got up, and walked over to the edge of the gorge and stood there, very still for a moment, facing left, just as the old bull had. He let his right arm hang in front of him, trunklike, hand moving in a small searching pattern. His left arm was crooked, hand to the side of his head, elbow flapping gently as big ears will to keep one cool. Then he shifted a little backward, adjusting his weight, and, in one smooth flowing turn, vanished amongst the rocks.

It was a brilliant performance. Not an impersonation, but a vivid evocation of elephantness. We never lost sight of the man, but we also never doubted for a moment that he was also an elephant. And in a flash we all understood that this was *his* elephant, an individual animal he knew well.

We clapped. He reappeared, made a little bow, and, pointing across the gorge, said something that sounded like *nau* except it was preceded by, and combined with, the sort of popping sound all small boys learn to make with their tongues to drive adults to distraction.

THERE are a thousand or more distinct languages in Africa, the world's most polyglot continent. These are extremely diverse, but fall into three main groups, corresponding roughly to the availability of Africa's most precious resource—water.

By far the largest group is the Niger-Congo tongues, originating in the tropical basins of these two west-flowing rivers. The second group is the Sub-Saharan, based on the marshes of Lake Chad or along the banks of the Upper Nile. The third group is a real curiosity.

Speakers of these languages may once have covered most of eastern and southern Africa, but are now cast out like stray splashes into the deserts of Namibia, the Kalahari, and the Karoo. Their numbers today are vanishingly small, but in the sixteenth century an estimated 300,000 of them still inhabited the Cape Coast and southwestern Africa, living in small groups of nomadic hunters and herders.

The origin of these people is obscure, but it is generally agreed they represent an aboriginal population. They were the first Africans, Stone Age hunters with bows and arrows who followed the herds, who followed the rains, and kept on doing so for tens of thousands of years.

They were small in stature, lightly built, with a sinewy strength. Their foreheads were flat and high, their cheekbones prominent, eyes deepset and narrow, with folds that were almost Oriental. Their skins were a coppery yellow, and, apart from sparse, tight peppercorn curls on their heads, they had little body hair. And their lifestyle left them with so little body fat that their skins wrinkled easily, making them look old before their time.

THERE were people exactly like these still living unobtrusively in the Cape when the first settlers arrived. The Dutch called them Bosjesmans or Bushmen, because they lived entirely by hunting and gathering and moved their makeshift camps every few weeks.

But there was also another group of local inhabitants, a little taller, more robust, more settled. They were pastoralists, owning herds of fat-tailed sheep and longhorned cattle, building encampments of beehive huts covered with woven grass mats, and moving these only when it was necessary to find new pastures.

The pastoral people, of course, looked down on their hunter neighbors, sometimes even employing them as servants. But recent archaeological evidence suggests that the pastoralists themselves descended from hunters who acquired domestic livestock several thousand years ago from communities of taller, darker farmers in the north, to whom they, in turn, were subservient.

The new herders called themselves Khoi ("Men") or Khoikhoi ("Real Men") and dismissed the hunters as San, a term whose origin remains obscure, but was probably derogatory and had something to do with having no cattle. And the hunters lived in such small groups, each with its own dialect, that they had no concept of a wider racial identity. But the Khoi and the San share so many physical and linguistic features, and are so different from all other Africans, that they have been grouped together now under the portmanteau name Khoisan.

These are the "click" speakers.

OUR visitor was one, and offered us whole mouthfuls of explosive clicking sounds. They seemed to us to involve the tongue a great deal and to come from the teeth, the roof of the mouth, and one or both cheeks. Each sharp sound was accompanied by a small rush of air into the mouth. Owl and I practiced a few as Starbuck looked on with embarrassment, but the best we could manage was a barnyard of clucks and gobbles that sounded more like poultry than people.

We needed help, and fortunately this was not the first time our new friend had been forced to deal with idiots.

He started his first lesson by shaking his head and saying *"Tsk, tsk, tsk,"* just like someone scolding us for doing badly. The sort of reproof we were used to hearing from teachers and parents. That was easy to do, just by putting the tip of your tongue behind the front upper teeth and pulling it away again.

We spent a few satisfying minutes rebuking each other for imaginary shortcomings—"Tsk, tsk."

Then he went *"Pop,"* making another sound we all knew. It is the one we had learned as children to imitate the sound of horses' hoofs on a hard surface. You do it by putting the front of your tongue up tight against the hard palate and pulling it away against the suction.

Starbuck got into the swing with this one, and the three of us soon had a whole herd in motion. And from that, by dropping your lower jaw to enlarge the mouth cavity, you can change the pitch of the sound and get a real *clip-clop* effect which is very impressive for beginners.

We practiced that for a while until he moved us on to the next sound, which doesn't involve the tongue at all and had the effect of getting all those noisy horses out of harm's way. You produce this by pulling one cheek sharply away from the back teeth on that side of the mouth, making a wetter sort of click. The kind of sound which riders everywhere still use to get their mounts going. Two little clicks in the cheek that mean "gee-up"—*gee gee*.

And finally he embarrassed everyone by pursing his lips at us and making the yucky *smack* sound of an air kiss. We didn't think we knew him well enough to go this far, but we batted our eyes at each other and went through the whole sequence of *tsk-pop-clip-clop-gee-gee-smack* until it became almost musical and picked up a cha-cha beat.

Before we knew what we were doing, Owl was leading us in a line dance back along the clifftop trail, pausing at the end of every seventh beat, then running through the refrain again and again. And our new dialect coach followed on, a little hesitantly, behind.

WHAT he had done, in less than half an hour, was to bridge the gap between the Stone Age and the New Age. In one simple phonetic lesson, he had accomplished more than the Dutch settlers managed in two centuries at the Cape. He had introduced us to the Khoisan linguistic speciality of a whole new subsystem of the usual consonants. The famous "clicks."

"Tsk-Pop-Clip-Clop-Gee-Gee-Smack" is a superficial, but very effective, kindergarten primer for the Khoisan alphabet. Professional linguists necessarily make much more of it with talk of audible friction, velar closures, imploding affricates, ingressive releases, and egressive aspirations. And there is a whole wide range of nasal sounds and glottal positions which introduce further subtleties. But basically there are just five clicks, which require a novel set of symbols that don't exist in any other language.

Tsk is now known as the dental click and is represented in written Khoisan as a forward-leaning slash: /

Pop is the palatal click, eloquently written as: !

Clip and **clop** are modified pops called alveolar clicks and recorded as a slash across an equal sign: ≠

Gee gee is the lateral click, shown as a double slash: //

And the **smack** of a kiss is the labial click, written simply as a period inside a zero: 0

Taken altogether, this combination of disapproval, horses' hoofs, whip cracks, gee-ups, and kisses tends to sound like a brush-fire. On paper it looks like printer's devils have taken over the press, but all these new signs are useful in that they already exist on the standard typewriter keyboard and are easily understood.

What they do is to offer anyone, anywhere, access to the wonderful world of the Khoisan.

So the soft pop that introduced our visitors comment on the old white bull would be written "*!Nau*," but we still didn't know what it meant, or even what his own name was.

I called a halt to the line dance and tried to carry out some belated introductions. And when all four of us were facing each other, I started again with our breakthrough word *buchu*, because that, it seems, was not just our name for the aromatic plant, but also his. It was a Khoisan word!

I made sniffing sounds, lifting my nose to indicate the act of smelling, and again said, "*Buchu*," pronouncing the word as he had, with the *ch* guttural as in Scottish "loch."

He nodded and, sniffing at his own arm, repeated: "*Buchu*." We were getting somewhere.

I took a chance and, pointing at his stick, I said, "Kierie"—the Afrikaans word for a fighting or hunting stick. He brandished it in affirmation and agreed that it was so: "*Kierie, kierie, kierie.*" Afrikaans is a made-up language, based on old Dutch but incorporating a lot of loan words from local languages, and it was clear that this was one of them.

I took another flier and pointed at his sheepskin cloak. In

Afrikaans, such a garment is known as a *kaross*. The *Oxford English Dictionary* defines it as "a mantle of animal skin used by South African tribesmen" and says the word is "of uncertain origin."

Without further prompting, he said, "*Kaross*," and made the origin clear. We now knew another Khoisan word.

I decided to return the favor immediately and pointed at my bespectacled friend, saying slowly, "Owl." And Owl helped things along by pointing at his own chest, saying, "Owl." Whereupon our tutor-turned-pupil, in perfect imitation, said, "Owl."

I pointed at myself, tapping my chest, and said my name: "Doc." He picked up on the routine very quickly, saying out loud "Doc."

It gave me a thrill, a burst of real pleasure, to hear him say it. So I rushed straight on and pointed at him, hoping it was not rude, and shrugging in a way I felt would indicate inquiry.

There was a moment of hesitation while he raised his hand and pointed, not at his chest, but at his nose. This surprised me then, but years later while in thrall to Desmond Morris, my tutor at the London Zoo, I learned that cultures do indentify themselves and the center of their being rather differently. Ask an Italian to indicate himself and he points at his stomach. Ask an Englishman and he points to his heart. Ask a Japanese, and he points invariably to the tip of his nose. Our new friend, who did look more Oriental than African, did exactly that, and then made my day.

With his fingertip tapping on his small, broad nose, he said proudly, "*Kamma*," and then "Kamma" again with just a hint of palatal click.

Now we knew. He was !Kamma.

THANKS to Sir Laurens van der Post, the Discovery Channel, and a cult film called *The Gods Must Be Crazy* involving a "Bushman"

and a Coca-Cola bottle, the image of the San is now recognized worldwide. They have had a good press, and recent research on their rock art has revealed an astonishing degree of religious and cultural sophistication. There may be only a small number of true San left, leading marginal lives in Botswana and Namibia, but who now knows anything about the Khoi?

The colonial name Hottentot persists, largely as the insult it was always intended to be. The Dutch considered them beastly, lazy, and degraded, useless savages who "neither dig nor spin." And the English seemed to agree. In 1726, Philip Stanhope, the fourth Earl of Chesterfield and a renowned wit and courtier, condemned Samuel Johnson with the words "The utmost I can do for him is to consider him a respectable Hottentot." In the earl's defense, it has to be said that Dr. Johnson had already criticized him as having "the morals of a whore and the manners of a dancing master." But even now, in a new and more enlightened millennium, it is hard to find anyone with a good word for "Hottentots."

The truth is that they were "Bushmen" whose greater height and weight were due to a diet of milk and meat. They were simply hunters who had adapted very well to a pastoral economy, and nomads with more worldly goods because they had draft oxen to carry them when they moved.

The two groups interacted frequently. There was an "upward" cycle of contacts between Khoi and San in which herders traded with the hunters for honey and skins, fought with them over hunting grounds, and took San women as additional wives. And there was a "downward" phase in which Khoi outcasts, usually widows without livestock, joined the San.

The Khoi had strong clan relationships, with captains, headmen, chiefs, and overlords, each step up the hierarchy involving larger huts, more body grease (animal fat was a luxury), and greater weight. The clans were more loosely affiliated into tribes, each bearing a traditional name such as Hessequa ("Those of the Woods"), Chainoqua

("Those with Round Faces"), and Outeniqua ("Those Who Collect Honey"). Authority in such groups was flexible. There were no standing armies and no military leaders. Disputes were settled by skirmishes with spears, often involving the innovative use of oxen as flying wedges to trample on opponents. And there was a pattern of shifting alliances amongst the tribes, depending on the most recent differences and vendettas, usually over water sources or women.

THE Khoi were not parochial. They traveled enough to have a good knowledge of other people. They traded with tribes in the interior for things like copper and iron, but geographically they were cut off from the rest of Africa by mountains and deserts, and from the rest of the world by vast oceans. They were not ready for the arrival of Europeans in the sixteenth and seventeenth centuries.

Occasional stopovers by traders bound for the Orient were disturbing, sometimes useful, having little long-term effect except perhaps a switch from ivory armbands to copper bracelets. But the permanent Dutch settlement changed everything. Within just seventy years from 1652, the Khoi were reduced to a fraction of their original population and their traditional economic and political institutions had collapsed.

The rapid decline of the Khoikhoi nation was as mysterious to the colonists as it still remains for us. It is a sad story without heroes, real villains, or redeeming features. The transformation was the result not of war or disease, but of cultural erosion.

To survive, the Khoi needed to keep possession of their cattle, to retain their traditional pastures, to be free to make their own decisions, and to maintain their own living standards. But the Dutch made that impossible. They absorbed livestock, encroached on pastures, subjugated the Khoi to Dutch law, and seduced local labor.

Without their herds, traditional leaders lost their prestige, pastoral-ists were compelled to work instead in the colony for food, tobacco, and liquor, and the European subjugation of southern Africa had begun.

Today there are no Khoi on the Cape Coast. No pastoral peo-ple to follow the rains. The tribes have been disbanded or dis-avowed by those anxious to sidestep apartheid and to be classified anything but "black." There has been such a premium attached to lightness of skin that, starting in the eighteenth century, a whole community of people of mixed origin came into being, proudly describing themselves as Bastards or Basters. They have become so successful and prosperous, trading and farming, buying land, even setting up their own regiments to serve in several wars, that they eventually resurrected the Khoi tribal identity of Gouriquas or Griquas. Only to face the ultimate irony in post-apartheid South Africa of being denied the right to belong to the far blacker new ruling majority.

Half a century ago, Dutch-born Dr. Hendrik Verwoerd had just become Minister of Native Affairs in South Africa and was busy leg-islating for complete separation of the races.

Blissfully unaware of these machinations and with only a vague understanding of history, we self-styled Strandlopers still somehow knew that !Kamma was very special, someone who had slipped through the net of discrimination and magically survived intact. We rushed him back to meet the rest of the band.

Our volunteer lookout, on that day one of the new kids, must have been half asleep at his post and missed the three of us at the head of the procession, catching just a glimpse of !Kamma in his sheepskin coming through the trees. He did a double-take and tumbled off his perch on Red Roman Rocks, running across the beach, shouting: "Pirates! Pirates! Pirates!"

Several Strandlopers appeared from different directions, look-ing first bemused, then incredulous, as we all came into view. The

Rock was the first to gather his wits with a quiet "Bloody Hell!" before coming up to meet us at the hut. And the rest followed on until the entire tribe was assembled, all looking at !Kamma with wide eyes.

He was the only one who seemed to be completely at ease, looking from face to face with real curiosity. We never did find out where he came from, what brought him here, or how he had managed to sidestep half the twentieth century, but there was no sign of uncertainty at this turn of events, no doubt or indecision in his bearing. He simply took charge.

He stepped into the center of the circle and, standing there in his skins, flung out his right arm like the ringmaster at a circus, pointed directly at me, and, with a voice that could have been my own, said: "Doc!"

He did the same for Owl and Starbuck, catching the tone of each of their voices with perfect pitch, and then, pointing at his own nose, he said proudly: "!Kamma."

We were captivated.

He carried right on, pointing next at the Rock, whom he had unerringly identified as our elder. The Rock caught on immediately, touching his own chest and calling out his name, which !Kamma repeated carefully and filed away. He did precisely the same with everyone there, stumbling only over Blossom, the name we had, rather cruelly, given to our lookout, a ten-year-old who had a small floral birthmark on his shoulder. But !Kamma never forgot the name or failed to reproduce the voice of any one of us.

We struggled a bit with his name, but none of us, not even for a moment, had any difficulty in accepting him as a fellow member. More than that, we felt somehow that he came to us as a visiting dignitary, someone holding high office in the global headquarters of Strandlopers Unlimited.

A founder.

!KAMMA joined us for a dinner of rock mussels that night, but as soon as it was over, melted away into the dunes.

He was back before first light, sitting quietly in front of the hut waiting for us to get on with the business of the day. As far as we were concerned, it was business as usual—forage, fish, fetch water—but he had other ideas.

!Kamma let us sort ourselves out, getting the day underway, but before we could settle into our normal routine, he took over. With authority and without warning, he stood up, cupped his hands around his mouth, and produced a strident call that stopped us in our tracks.

It was a high-frequency squeal that increased in volume until it broadened into a scream which echoed across the entire bay. The unmistakable trumpet call of an adult elephant, demanding attention.

He got it.

THERE are arguments still about exactly how an elephant does it. The general feeling is that "trumpeting" is simply the result of air being blown through the trunk. The French even call an elephant's trunk *trompe*, which means trumpet; but that begs the question. The sound is certainly modified by the length and shape of the trunk, as it is in any wind instrument, but new sonic research suggests that there is more to it. There appears to be a vocal component, a sound produced in the well-developed larynx, which begins as a squeak or a squeal at high amplitude and then resonates through the trunk. Elephants with trunks cut short by snares or crocodiles have trouble trumpeting in tune.

!Kamma somehow circumvented the whole problem and relied

entirely on his voice to do the job. He held every eye and kept our attention focused on him all the way down to the shore, putting his feet carefully in place, measuring every step as he slid down the dune, braking as necessary, picking up heft as he went, until by the time he hit the beach he had four columnar legs and a trunklike arm with which he tested the air.

We watched in delight as he shambled across the sand, stopping to examine things, picking up a piece of driftwood, juggling with it, curling his trunk to taste it before flinging it aside, flapping an ear-like arm, making a little mock charge at a kelp gull that stood in his path, waggling his head in amusement, getting closer and closer to the water, slowing down as he did so, the gait more tentative, reaching out to test the nature of the waves ahead . . . and then stopping.

He was all elephant now, curious but not convinced. One leg swinging to and fro in the throes of indecision, getting mixed signals on the air. It was water, but . . . Letting his trunk drop lower and closer until finally it touched the surface, sucking up a trial half gallon, swinging this nonchalantly around and then, as the saltiness registered, squirting it all out again with a wonderful hissy snort of disgust before reversing abruptly and turning his back on the sea. Standing finally a safe distance away, he ended his extraordinary riff with the sort of all-body shrug that only an elephant can fill with such complete and unquestionable disdain.

We got the message. He wasn't interested in the ocean. It was all right, in its own place. Interesting enough to listen to maybe, but what was it all for? !Kamma had other plans for us today. Something with elephants in it. . . .

FYNBOS, the unique plant kingdom of the Cape Coast, is a product of the ocean, a response to warm summers, wet winters, and the westerly airflow of the southern hemisphere. All winds here come off the sea, sweeping across the coastal plain, bumping sooner or later into a folded mountain chain. Air rises, cools, condenses, and rain falls in amounts directly proportional to the height of the barrier involved.

In the east, the Outeniqua Mountains reach six or seven thousand feet and precipitation is high enough to support an undergrowth of water-loving ferns and a canopy of dense indigenous forest. The dominant trees are hardwoods—ironwood, stinkwood, and yellowwood—growing up to 160 feet with trunks over forty feet in circumference. And it is their presence here that has attracted a timber industry, beginning in the eighteenth century and continuing still, giving rise to logging companies centered in the rapidly growing town of Knysna on the edge of a beautiful lagoon.

The forest once covered an area of three thousand square miles, but two centuries of wood-cutting for furniture, floors, wagons, boats, and even railway sleepers has reduced it now to less than a third of that area. It is still large enough, however, to provide a home for leopards and monkey, bushbuck and bushpig, lynxes and porcupines. But by the time I was born, the last of the great herd of buffaloes had gone, along with all but about a dozen of the Knysna elephants.

As children, we had been driven along the unpaved forest roads on our way to Plettenberg Bay and had thrilled to the sight and smell of large, fresh elephant droppings, left steaming in the cool morning air. I had insisted on the first occasion, at the age of five, on being allowed out of the car to get a closer look and had plunged my hands deep into the musty warmth of the heap to get as close to the giants as I could. And been forced to ride the rest of the way sitting on the wide running board of our old Packard.

We never saw a Knysna elephant. Very few people did. After being hounded for so long, they had learned to keep away from woodcutters and foresters, leading a secret life in the deep *kloofs* or wooded valleys, crossing roads only when necessary, after dark or after long periods hidden in the bushes on the verge until satisfied that no vehicles were anywhere near. The droppings we did encounter were left, it seems, in plain sight as a sort of elephantine joke, a defiant gesture, but I always accepted them as precious gifts.

By the time I became a Strandloper, most of the remaining forest was managed, under state or provincial control, subject to selective logging or set aside as nature reserve. Maps of it look like patchwork quilts, with a central area of dark virgin growth surrounded by blotches of big trees, some left standing only for easy access by visitors. And running right through the center of the forest, midway between the mountains and the sea, is the wide N2, now a major highway that parallels the coast, carrying all the traffic on the Cape's famous Garden Route.

Half a century ago, it was relatively quiet, the flow restricted by gates that had to be opened and closed, but the damage had been done and we no longer visited the forest much. It had lost some of its magic, but the section between the road and the sea was still intact and ran right down to the cliffs where we had seen the white bull. Word was that the elephants no longer crossed the highway to get to this area, so our sighting had been all the more wonderful, and I certainly had no qualms about going back to the gorge as !Kamma seemed to want to do.

So all but three of us, our usual hindguard, set out to do just that—and entered wonderland.

THE first thing you notice about Cape forest is that it is surprisingly quiet. With !Kamma leading the way, we walked inland along the near rim of the gorge, starting from where we had seen the great elephant, and soon moved out of the small-leafed shrubland into true high forest.

The canopy is made up partly of Cape ash with smooth bark in various shades of gray, drooping feathery leaves, and scented flowers. This is usually mixed with hard pear, a tree with creamy bark that flakes to reveal a pale orange skin. It has round red fruits that birds are crazy about. There were none in attendance that morning, but when something moved in the foliage overhead, !Kamma stopped and made a round *koo-koo-koo* call, slowly rising in volume and pitch and then dying away.

It was immediately answered from above, and soon we could see a large bird with a leaf-green body bouncing along, mounted almost on springs, making the lightest possible contact with each branch, climbing easily up to the highest perches. !Kamma engaged it in a brief dialogue, until he said the wrong thing and the bird took off and gave itself away. When it glides, the Knysna *lourie*, a kind of turaco, reveals a startling spread of crimson feathers on its wings.

We walked along a pig path through *quar*, trees of the gardenia family with fluted boles and glossy oval leaves, and a patch of stinkwood, a Knysna speciality much sought-after by furniture makers for its fine-textured, foul-smelling dark wood.

!Kamma passed all these glories by, but came to a halt in front of a huge tree, one big enough to rise up well above the canopy, towering majestically over its neighbors. It was giant yellowwood, tall as a fifteen-story building, straight enough to be used as the mainmast on a square-rigged sailing ship, with a shaggy crown of small sickle-shaped leaves on branches festooned with beards of lichen.

He stood there for a moment, head bowed, then put down his stick and bag and, for the first time since we had met him, took off his sheepskin *kaross*. Clad only in a brief loincloth, he circled the giant slowly, several times, one hand trailing to touch its smooth bark, muttering a sort of mantra spiked with more than its fair share of clicks. And then he moved in close, putting his bare back up against the mighty trunk, spreading his arms out wide, as far as he could reach in a sort of reverse hug, and stood there, head back with his eyes closed.

It was like looking at a small, dark Christ figure on a gigantic crucifix waiting for the word from above. We watched respectfully from a distance.

Minutes passed without a movement, without a sound. The grove around the big tree was absolutely silent. There were no crickets, no frogs, no flies. Not even a stray breath of air. It was like being in an empty cathedral.

I looked down around me, hoping for an ant, anything to break the spell and the growing suspicion that we were trapped in a frozen moment. The forest floor was clear for some yards around the buttress roots of the great yellowwood, swept almost clean over an area roughly the same size and shape as the crown high above. I thought about this and began to wonder if the tree had a sort of umbrella effect over its own feet, but then something else caught my eye. The ground around the tree was not swept so much as tamped down, and when I bent to take a closer look, what I saw was a pattern of overlapping shapes. Big shapes, round ones and oval ones, hundreds of them, neatly arranged around the tree, superimposed upon one another in endless concentric circles, like scales on a fish or on a butterfly's wing. And then it hit me. . . .

They were footprints! Elephant footprints. All left by the same adult elephant walking slowly round the tree, clockwise, just as !Kamma had done.

ELEPHANTS make trails. When walking, elephants "pace," placing their hind feet on the spot each forefoot fell. They almost coincide and leave a trail far narrower than one might expect.

They also tend to follow each other in single file along the same paths again and again, wearing these down in a way that creates "elephant walks" so sensitive to contours that they are often followed by highway engineers. And they may travel in circles, showing great reluctance to deviate from such chosen paths, but I had never heard of an elephant, other than in confinement in a circus or a zoo, walking so tight a circle as this one around a single tree. And I was prepared to bet that the prints I was looking at there were those of the white bull. They had precisely the same patterns as !Kamma had drawn for us the previous day.

I looked up at him still pressed against the tree, and as I did, he moved. He opened his eyes, wide, and said one word. The same word he had used at the gorge when we first met. The one with a palatal click.

"*!Nau.*"

He stepped briskly away from the tree, picked up his *kaross*, and smiled brightly at us. We looked at each other.

"*!Nau,*" he said again.

Right now? What? Who? We shrugged.

All he did was cup a hand to his ear. Listen!

We listened. Nothing.

We listened to him listening. Still nothing.

He turned to look toward the far side of the glade, and then we heard it too.

Actually, it was something you felt rather than heard. A trembling in the air. The sort of flutter that you picked up in your chest. We looked at each other and everyone seemed to feel the same thing. It was nothing any of us had ever knowingly felt before, but every one of us knew what it meant.

An elephant was coming!

MANY of those who have had the good fortune of getting close to elephants in the wild know this feeling.

Joyce Poole, working at Amboseli in the 1980s, came to feel that she could tell when there were elephants nearby and trusted this feeling well enough for it to guide her daily research activity. It was not anything she could hear or smell or see, just that "if elephants were absent, the landscape had a stillness, an emptiness." But if elephants were anywhere nearby, "there seemed to be a vibrancy in the air, a certain warmth."

As a child, of course, I knew nothing of this, but the feeling was very strong. We found ourselves closing ranks behind !Kamma and looking in the same direction. He held up a hand to keep us quiet, to tell us to stay still. We did.

For a long while, nothing happened. !Kamma turned his head slowly from side to side, like a radar dish scanning for incoming information. We heard nothing, but then, suddenly, we could feel it beneath our bare feet. A gentle throb, a faint but measured beat as though we were standing on a sprung dance floor or feeling for a pulse in someone else's chest.

We all sensed it and exchanged anxious glances. It was coming our way. . . .

!Kamma began to move slowly forward across the glade to meet it, picking his feet up high and putting them back down slowly, avoiding every twig and leaf. We followed on, a little less expertly but doing the best we could, until we could all see past the big tree and down the incoming trail.

There is seldom any breeze on the forest floor, but at that moment a gentle waft of air brought news of something different. Something organic, yet unlike the usual cool smell of plant decay. The warm scent of elephant!

We waited, wondering if there were trees nearby we could climb in a hurry if necessary. There didn't seem to be, and my mind turned to thoughts of things far less dignified. To the idea of running away; and even if we did, to the question of whether two legs really were better than four. I doubted it.

The tremble in the air was now a solid tremor, strong enough to register on the Richter scale. It seemed to surround us, but there was still nothing to see. Not a leaf moved, not a bird called, but not one of us doubted that we had company.

It is hard to believe that something weighing ten tons, carrying unwieldy columns of ivory over six feet long, breathing ten times a minute, having a seventy-pound heart that beats every two seconds and a stomach fueled by three hundred pounds of fresh green fuel producing three hundred gallons of methane a day, maintaining over two hundred square feet of rough skin in contact with the environment while dealing at the same time with another three hundred pounds of restless trunk—could ever be silent even for a second. But it can. We didn't move a muscle for what must have been several minutes, and never heard a sound.

Not until a wall of rumpled, unexpectedly pale skin metamorphosed out of the shadows around a large white-ringed, yet benign, eye with astonishing lashes. To begin with, it had no form or locus, but as we looked, it became an indisputable part of an enormous elephant just feet away. The old white bull had been standing there for goodness knows how long, barely concealed by the sparse leaves of a candlewood tree.

With our hearts in our mouths, we looked at him looking at us, unable to move, unable even to breathe or to do anything sensible. And then he moved, making another of his eerie exits, drifting away into nothing without a sound.

KATY PAYNE, who pioneered the study of elephant sounds, draws attention also to their silence, marveling at the ability of even a herd of elephants with young calves to keep completely quiet when this is called for.

Iain and Oria Douglas-Hamilton frequently found that herds of up to a hundred elephants would materialize like magic around their Tanzanian camp: "Suddenly, out of nowhere, the whole riverbed was covered with elephants and none of us had heard them come."

Joyce Poole describes shy Kilimanjaro elephants, well known for their ability to just "disappear into thin mountain air."

This is made possible, for a start, by the construction of their feet. The digits of each limb are so steeply angled that elephants walk almost on tiptoe with a very pliant step. Behind each heel lies a large spongy pad of fatty tissue that not only supports the fingers and toes, but distributes the great body weight evenly across the wide horny sole of the foot. This inner sole forms a shock-absorbing cushion that behaves like a lightly inflated tire. When the foot is lifted, it bulges from the underside, but as soon as it is set down, the pad splays out and smothers leaves and twigs beneath it, muffling sound and giving even these giant animals an elastic step and the stealth of a cat.

All of which makes sense, but their use of this soft slipper is uncanny.

Many years later, reluctantly, I learned the lesson of silence.

It wasn't easy. Western awareness insists on things as the focus of sensation. We find it very hard to think of nothing. Emptiness makes us uncomfortable. Silence is, more often than not, interrupted by thoughtless applause from someone who thinks the symphony is over. We are all a little anxious about intervals, finding it very difficult to foster the art of the meaningful pause. We do our best to abolish empty space, dead air, filling it instead with clutter, forgetting that it is precisely the nothingness between things that defines them, setting them apart from one another.

We need to stop talking and listen. Learn to listen to silence, because the secrets often lie in the spaces between the sounds. The sounds of silence.

Oriental and African notions of time and music give equal value to object and interval. By accepting space as an area of change and expression, they create new rhythms. It doesn't matter that intervals, by their very nature, are incomplete. This helps to invite participation, allowing us to immerse ourselves, not in notes or other concrete things, but in the silences in between.

I believe that !Kamma knew this and was trying to tell us about it by urging us to listen to him listening to nothing.

WE had heard nothing and seen altogether too much and didn't know what to do with ourselves until Owl broke the spell with a nervous burst of laughter. The rest of us, when we could finally collect our wits, all started to talk at once. Blossom burst into tears.

It was hard to take in. We had walked into a primeval forest with an aboriginal guide, armed with nothing but our walking sticks. We had found a giant tree, standing alone, serving it seemed as some sort of shrine or antenna.

We had watched our tutor, apparently entranced, use the yellowwood to summon up a great elephant at will. And we had stood there in the spooky grove as this force of nature had come undetected to within inches of us, taking our measure and then just melting away again.

What do you do with an experience like that? What does it

mean? Who can you tell? Had it actually happened? Was the elephant real, or had we imagined the whole thing? We were all young and inexperienced in such things, and turned in the end to !Kamma for advice. But to our horror, he was gone. The glade was empty.

We turned as one and ran, shamelessly, away.

Panic is infectious. Boetie had the fastest start, sprinting back down the path in fine form, elbows pumping. Blossom was close in his wake, crashing along through the ferns, making a noise that spurred Boetie on to even greater lengths. The rest vied for third place in a pack centered on Owl, and the Rock and I brought up the rear, each of us casting backward glances when the other got a little ahead. I don't remember much else about our ignominious retreat, but it ended with all of us tumbling out of the forest and collapsing in a heap once we were well away out in the open.

And there, of course, was !Kamma, magically transported from the big tree, sitting on a rock beside the gorge with a wide grin on his wrinkled face.

He didn't hold it against us. Running away, after all, is one of the essential survival skills. Sometimes it is the only sensible thing to do. But that didn't stop him from reenacting our panic-stricken rout for the benefit of the rest of the band back at our evening campfire.

They loved it and called for several encores.

!Kamma obliged, but then he introduced a new note. Something that seemed to grow naturally out of our adventure of the day. It was a dark, cloudless night, and he began to tell us, entirely with sounds and gestures, Khoi stories about the stars.

He started with the Pleiades, the famous Seven Sisters clustered into a question mark near the horns of Taurus, which I pointed to with the help of a flashlight beam that hung easily in the cool sea air. These he said were /huseti, with a tsk sound, indicating that it meant a group of people, like ourselves, brought together for such an occasion.

Then he pointed to Orion, which we know as the Hunter, and singled out the conspicuous belt of three bright stars by punching three holes in the sand with his stick. These, he explained, with an evocatively rounded imitation of animals with stripes, were !goregu—the Three Zebras—plump with new life and hope for the herd.

Drawing a sweeping line across the sky with his stick, he focused on the two bright Pointers, the stars that indicate where the Southern Cross can be found, and called these *xami di mura*—The Eyes of the Lion—he who watches everything and pounces on stragglers or anyone isolated and made vulnerable by being alone.

And he ended his astronomy lesson by drawing our attention to the Milky Way, that great arc of stars and dust that represents most of the rest of our galaxy, seen in depth. The Khoi, it seems, know this as *tsaob*, which means the Embers—a fact he made clear by scattering some of the coals from the edge of the campfire.

Out on the sand, these glowed briefly, but cut off from the collective warmth of the hearth, soon winked out, and as the last one lost its light, he touched it with the tip of his stick and I heard him say softly, "!Kamma."

ELEPHANTS lead extraordinarily complex social lives.

Females, in particular, are never alone. They are born into and live in bonded groups which they never leave. These groups, in turn, enjoy the experience of a multitiered network of other elephants, encompassing finally an entire local population who live in a far-flung herd.

As a rule, all the members of a family group eat, drink, rest, and travel at the same time, keeping constant contact with one another, calling, sniffing, touching tusks and trunks, tasting each other's mouths, interacting, in Katy Payne's words, "like ants which exchange drops of regurgitated liquid when they meet, and so learn about the composition and condition of the colony."

All elephants greet each other, but when the encounter involves members that are directly related, the reunion is effusive. Cynthia Moss, who followed one family in Amboseli for thirteen years, describes it as thrilling. "The two subgroups of the family will run together, rumbling, trumpeting, and screaming, raise their heads, click their tusks together, entwine their trunks, flap their ears, spin around and back into each other, urinate and defecate, and generally show great excitement. A greeting such as this will sometimes last for as long as ten minutes." A concert which obviously serves to reinforce old bonds.

Similar rituals and ceremonies cement relationships all the way up the scale from families to groups through clans and on to encompass every elephant in an ecosystem. Mature males lead slightly different lives, compelled by testosterone and musth (an Urdu word that means "sexual intoxication") to seek the company of others like themselves. Not as rogues or outsiders, but as vital satellites to the female herds. They too keep in touch, by sound and smell, because where elephants are concerned, nothing less than the whole community is real.

A solitary elephant is not an elephant at all.

This I know now, but even as an apprentice Strandloper, I worried about !Kamma and the white elephant. They had a lot in common. Without their herds, they were lost.

CHAPTER THREE

Finding the Elephant

The proper study of mankind
is man, but when one regards
the elephant, one wonders.
–Alexander Pope in *An Essay on Man,* 1734

ELEPHANTS and humans have much in common.

We go back a long way. Back to fossil roots in Africa, to basic mammals not far removed from the original pattern. And each of us, about ten million years ago, took a decisive turn, one that produced modifications which still identify our species today.

In that shake-up, ancestral elephants got a new set of teeth. Molars formed from hard grinding enamel and a softer tooth cement, so that the two parts wore down at different rates, keeping the chewing surface from becoming too smooth. With such ever-ready grinders, modern elephants are able to deal with tougher foods like woody shrubs, making it possible for them to live in more barren habitats.

Our ancestors went through a similar adaptive change, becoming more omnivorous, more gregarious, growing larger, radiating out in ways that prepared them for the same dry times in which forests shrank and made way for the savanna.

And, starting around two or three million years ago, all of our founding fathers were beset by another major climatic change, the trial by winter of the Ice Age. Over large areas of the planet, snow fell faster than it melted.

Year by year it accumulated into glaciers, and deserts expanded in front of the ice sheets, changing the geography and the nature of life everywhere.

The response of elephants and hominids was the same. We began to wander, traveling literally to the ends of the earth. As the climate changed, so did we, reacting to the "Goldilocks Effect," moving more to the center of adaptation. Not too large or too small, but just right. Giant *Mammuthus* came out of the forests of central Africa to explore Eurasia as the sleeker, more mobile *Elephas*, which led to the Asian elephant. And gracile *Australopithecus* descended from the trees of eastern Africa as a larger, more robust member of our genus *Homo*, better able to exploit the new possibilities of another continent.

WE were not alone. Over forty species of elephantids competed and coexisted with perhaps a dozen early hominids, the struggle narrowing slowly down to *Homo erectus*, our immediate ancestor, versus *Mammuthus primigenius*, the woolly mammoth.

Red, hairy elephants were an important part of life on the way into the Ice Ages. Our contact with them has been vividly recorded in cave paintings at Pech Merle and La Madeleine in southern France that feature shaggy elephants with extraordinarily domed foreheads and sloping backs, some clearly at bay, riddled with spears. They were thick-skinned, small-eared animals, well adapted to winter, with wildly curved fifteen-foot tusks that may well have served as snow plows. And they survived until less than four thousand years ago, holding out on Wrangel Island in the Siberian Arctic until 1500 B.C., succumbing finally to the combined effects of hunting and habitat destruction. But they carry on, at least as enduring legends, in the minds and mystical heritage of many northern people.

There were reports of "large hairy elephants" beyond the Ural Mountains as recently as the sixteenth century, sparked perhaps by the discovery of frozen mammoths rising from the ice in a spring thaw. And several even more recent accounts in the twentieth century from Tunguskan hunters of "enormous elephants with white, very curved tusks" still leaving heaps of steaming dung scattered across the Siberian taiga.

THAT would be wonderful, but for all practical purposes, there are only two genera of elephants left: *Elephas* in Asia and *Loxodonta* in Africa. This, however, is enough to demonstrate some fascinating evolutionary diversions.

The two surviving groups of elephant differ in several ways: Asian elephants are smaller and lighter, seldom more than eight feet tall or over three tons. African elephants stand up to eleven feet at the shoulder and can weigh ten tons. The Asian species has smaller ears and shorter tusks, and females are always tuskless, while all elephants in Africa can have large, sometimes extravagantly large, tusks up to 220 pounds on each side. The trunks of African elephants are also more segmented and have two fingerlike projections at the tip, instead of the Asian elephant's one.

In profile, African elephants are clearly more robust, more angular, with rumps higher than their sway backs and massive heads with very large ears. The Asian is generally more gently rounded, with two small domes on its forehead and far smaller, blotchy ears. There are variations too in their teeth—*Loxodonta* has molars with lozenge-shaped patterns—but the most obvious differences lie in their temperament, and in the history of their relationships with humans.

IN Asia, elephants and humans seem to have lived together in a form of partnership for thousands of years. And yet, over a hundred people are killed by elephants every year in India alone, most of them by bulls in musth on forest paths created and used by the elephants themselves.

In more sparsely populated Africa, there has traditionally been far less direct contact between humans and elephants, and a correspondingly lower level of fatalities as a result of elephant attacks. But despite this, in most of Africa, elephants are widely feared, while in all of Southeast Asia, they continue to be just as widely revered.

Religion may have something to do with these contradictory responses. Elephants figure prominently in the Hindu pantheon. Airavata, the mount of Indra, god of rain and thunder, is depicted as an elephant; as were Mahapadma ("Great Forest") and Saumanesa ("Keeper of Soma"), who bore the entire earth on their massive shoulders. And Ganesh ("Lord of Beginnings") is honored as a demigod bearing the head of an elephant with one broken tusk, an injury suffered defending Shiva from attack.

Buddhists believe that the birth of Gautama himself took place as a result of the impregnation of the chaste and virginal Queen Sirimahamaya by the trunk of a divine elephant. And a white elephant stands in the center of the flag of old Siam and is venerated in Laos and Burma as one of the Buddha's many animal reincarnations. So elephants were domesticated for largely ritual purposes in all of Indochina, beginning four thousand years ago in the Indus Valley, where they were celebrated for their nobility and faithfulness. But it is true too that, right from the start of this relationship, elephants were also valued as draft animals, beasts of burden, and as mounts on the front lines in times of war.

Armored elephants were used by Aryan generals three thousand years ago, as spearheads that led horses and chariots into an attack, throwing enemy ranks into disarray. In the third century B.C., the king of Epirus took Macedonia and crossed the Adriatic Sea to inflict "Phyrric" victories on Rome with the help of war elephants, each said to be the military equivalent of six thousand horses. And seventeenth-century battles between Moguls and Hindus, Persians and Turks, all involved elephants. Some of them, crazed by alcohol, were even persuaded to execute prisoners by crushing their heads on a block.

COMPARED to this, the African response of relative indifference seems benign.

It was not that African elephants were intractable. Hannibal's famous attack on Rome in 218 B.C. was led by thirty-seven very well trained elephants, most of which were African. Sub-Saharan attitudes to elephants were just different. Where Asians, for whatever reason, valued *live* elephants. most Africans preferred them *dead*— as mountains of meat. But out on the savanna there was an abundance of other game animals, ones far easier to catch and kill, so there was little point in pursuing more dangerous elephants.

And it was not that Africans don't like elephants. Myth and religion on the continent are deeply rooted in the world of nature, drawing most often on animals such as lions, jackals, baboons, and meerkats—none of which are normally eaten. And while it is true that elephants play a very minor role in tribal folklore and superstition, this is largely because African elephants could, and still do whenever possible, keep their distance, preferring to retreat rather than compete. People accepted that separation, acknowledging the strength and presence of elephants, without ever considering the idea of establishing a closer bond.

Elephants in most of Africa were never involved in domestication or warfare or hunting for food as long as they didn't interfere with pastoral or agricultural activities. It was a case of live and let be. The difference between African and Asian attitudes to elephants boils down in the end to this: Asians deify and enslave their elephants, while Africans respect and kill theirs. Neither is good news for proboscids, but there was one group of Africans who had a very different relationship with them.

STARTING about ten thousand years ago, when the Ice Age was over and the Sahara was a place of shallow lakes and green marshes, elephants and humans came into direct contact.

The humans were hunters, but as far as we can tell, they hunted mainly antelope and wild sheep. They recorded such hunts in rock paintings and engravings in the mountains of what are now Algeria, Libya, and Chad. But they also created a gallery of large, bold, very lifelike portraits of elephants. African elephants drawn from life, waggling their heads, flapping their big ears, making the sort of floppy runs that are typical of proboscids at play. Groups of elephants gathered in greeting ceremonies, mothers protecting their calves from attacks by lions, and solitary males standing tall and thoughtful in the shade of a tree.

These talented artists disappeared around eight thousand years ago as the Sahara dried up, but their practices resurfaced at the other end of Africa in the sophisticatd rock art of the southern "Bushmen," the San.

Southern Africa is the home of the largest open-air art gallery in the world. Painted on the walls of rock shelters in the mountains and engraved on every suitable surface all across the plains are true works of art.

In form, line, and composition, they astound. In number, they exceed anything to be found anywhere else. The Rock Art Register at the South African Museum now lists nearly five thousand separate sites with over 100,000 subjects, and more are being discovered every year. All of which is exciting, but it is in intellectual content that this southern tradition excells.

Like the Saharan scenes, they include subtle portrayals of animal and human figures involving careful foreshortening, a skillful use of perspective, and shaded polychrome compositions of tremendous sensitivity in red ocher, orange and yellow earth colors, white lime, and black charcoal—all fixed, it seems, by egg white. But there is more. The southern works also involve complex overlay and superimposition, extraordinary mythological figures, caricatures, and elaborate geometric designs. They are carefully constructed statements.

Early opinion dismissed this art as the doodlings of bored black herdboys. More careful later examination led to a variety of theories—including art for art's sake, simple decoration, sympathetic hunting magic, historical narrative, and even messages from passing Phoenicians. But none of these suggestions accounts for the fact that the artists were highly selective and repetitive in their choice of subjects, and meticulous in the way they allowed these to interact. The art is symbolic rather than narrative. Nothing is quite what it seems, but it took a German linguist in the nineteenth century and an English teacher in the twentieth century to crack the code.

Wilhelm Bleek emigrated to the Cape in 1855 to compile

another Zulu grammar, but was soon diverted by the discovery that no one had yet made any kind of study of the San languages.

He took a job as a court translator and was given permission to interview San convicts imprisoned, as Nelson Mandela was to be a century later, on Robben Island. That was a brave thing to do in a society which considered the little people to be degenerate and useless, but he persisted and was eventually allowed to take several San out of the prison to live with him as   servants in his Cape Town home.

One of these was a grizzled older man called //Kabbo, whom Bleek described as "a gentle old soul, lost in a dream-life of his own." A life he was more than happy to talk about in stories and folklore which Bleek transcribed over five years, translating and recording everything in a series of notebooks that eventually stretched, with the help of his wife, Jemima, and her sister, Lucy Lloyd, to twelve thousand numbered pages of texts, word lists, and notes. These provided the basis for a San dictionary as well as a profound view of a way of life that was already vanishing when Bleek died in 1875.

The Bleek collection ended up in the Jagger Library at the University of Cape Town, where it was of only limited academic interest until 1974. In that year, David Lewis-Williams spent three months reading through the entire collection. "I had to keep reminding myself," he said, "that these were the actual notebooks that had lain on the table between //Kabbo and Bleek." Books the shaman //Kabbo had held and hoped would fulfill his desire to give the San stories to the world.

Lewis-Williams realized that the notebooks could well do that, and a lot more. The folklore that //Kabbo had dictated was an account of the dreams, preoccupations, and aspirations of the San themselves, the people whose ancestors made the rock art. The notebooks, he believed, could be the "Rosetta Stone" necessary to decipher the intent and the meaning of the enigmatic paintings.

They were. In the following years, Lewis-Williams produced a flurry of papers and books that promised not only to reveal the secrets of rock art in South Africa but to open new doors to the study of parietal art everywhere. He parlayed his discovery and enthusiasm into a new chair at the University of the Witwatersrand in Johannesburg, where he became the world's first Professor of Cognitive Archaeology and soon gathered around him a team of researchers in what is now a well-respected Rock Art Research Institute.

THANKS to //Kabbo, it is now possible to understand that the rock paintings mean far more than they seem to depict. The key to the art lies in rituals and metaphors. Looked at in this way, the paintings become what Lewis-Williams calls "icons fulfilling a symbolic function." They are associated with the ritual activities of shamans, special people who exorcised illness, made rain, and controlled the movements of game.

Where women are seen to be using sticks weighted with bored stones at one end, they are not just digging for succulent roots on the veld. According to //Kabbo, those same stones are beaten on the ground as a way of calling upon the spirits. In San minds, the sacred and the profane are often indistinguishable.

When a painting appears to depict a dead eland, the chances are that the antelope is actually a shaman in animal form during trance, undergoing the "little death" that allows him to act as an intermediary between the waking world and the spirit world.

Circling dancers are not just having a good time, they are far more likely to be using the dance rhythm as a means of entering an altered state of consciousness in which they often bleed from their noses. And a white line linking figures, animal and human, in any scene is not a rope used to restrain livestock or slaves, but an esoteric artery along which power moves when a shaman is successful in summoning up the energy of the earth itself.

Viewed in this way, it becomes clear that the paintings are partly records of shamanic experience, partly celebrations of the way in which the spirit world blends with and informs daily life, and partly spiritual weapons designed to protect the people against malevolence in any form. Their beauty, their complexity, and their abundance are all measures of the reverence in which the San hold the land. And even in the absence of the artists, most of southern Africa remains consecrated, a country decorated with many thousands of Stone Age shrines.

Some of them depict elephants. Not elephants being hunted or killed in the manner of mammoths in much European rock art. Nor elephants standing in for "rain animals" in rituals designed to break a drought. But elephants unadorned, complete in their elephantness, complex, compassionate, and deeply involved in one another.

It is no coincidence that such inspiration bears fruit now even in the coat of arms of the new Republic of South Africa. It carries a motto in the old San language *!ke e: /xarra //ke*, "Those who are different, joining together."

HALF a century before such amity, at age twelve, I struggled to make sense of our own small miracle on the beach.

In just two days, !Kamma had turned our world upside down. He had come out of nowhere, appearing in the same time and place as a big pale elephant, with whom he seemed to have a strange bond.

We thought at first we had adopted him, but it soon became obvious it was the other way around. He had collected us under the wing of his *kaross* and, step by step, was trying to teach us something important. Something we needed to know, but were slow to grasp.

We were, after all, a motley collection of young boys, all white, all brought up in a society which wore blinkers. One which clung desperately to the idea of empire and the supremacy of our northern race, loving Africa but holding it at arm's length, never letting it get too close, afraid of what might happen once we dropped our guard.

Our only saving grace, it seemed, was the existence of the hut and our sojourn there as Strandlopers. But that was a giant step. It set us apart from our contemporaries and forced us to look at ourselves and our surroundings in a different way. It freed us, even if only for a month each year, from the constraints and the preoccupations of our parents. It brought us closer to Africa than they knew, or would otherwise have allowed. It was a window on another world.

THE morning of our third day with !Kamma started quietly enough. It was one of those magical Cape summer days without wind. The air was cool and clear, there wasn't a cloud in sight, and the sea was so calm it was impossible to tell where ocean ended and sky began.

The Rock was up early as usual and out on the rocks pitting his wits against a *leervis*, a member of the jackfish family with a high fin and ladderlike markings down each side. It is recognized as South Africa's best all-around game fish and renowned for its strength and cunning. It is a predator, interested only in live bait, preferably mullet, which it seems to scale with its teeth before swallowing. The trick is to attract one and then exercise extraordinary patience.

The *leervis*, in its first move, passes quickly by, stunning its prey with one blow from its large tail. You do nothing. It comes back about twenty or thirty seconds later and starts to mouth the bait, working it to and fro in its jaws. You wait. Then it takes the bait and makes a trial run, tearing line off your reel for twenty yards or more. Still you wait; one hint of resistance and the *leervis* leaves. Finally the big fish settles down, working its meal again, taking the strain, getting it into position to be swallowed whole, headfirst. You count slowly up to ten and then you make your move. You strike: and commit yourself to a battle with a fighting fish that may weigh almost as much as you do.

Owl and Starbuck were less keen on fishing. They were working their way through shrubbery at the head of the beach, each with a container in hand, something found at the tideline and large enough to hold a field cricket. These insects with big eyes are tireless singers on warm evenings, rubbing their hind wings together to attract females, modulating the sound by alternately amplifying and smothering it with the forewings. They confuse predators by such acts of ventriloquism, but met their match in our two hunters, who needed them for another reason. The crickets were part of our weather service. If you count the number of chirps they make each minute, subtract 40, divide by 4, and add 50, the result is the air temperature in degrees Fahrenheit.

Not having wristwatches, we measured the passage of each minute by counting out the seconds in "chimpanzees"— an approximate method, but it did give us a rough idea of changes from day to day.

Boetie was busy sorting out his collection of twine and cord, all washed ashore, making it up into lengths suitable for traps that required a trigger line. And !Kamma and I were just sitting on a log in front of the hut watching all this measured activity going on, enjoying the sight and sound of a tribe in action, making a living for themselves.

Out of the corner of my eye, I was also keeping track of one of my favorite spiders. It is less than half an inch wide, with a smooth glistening body, mottled in white and gray to look exactly like a bird dropping, still wet, freshly made. This not only protects it from pre-dation by birds, but allows it to leap on butterflies that are normally attracted to bird droppings for the salts they contain. For the moment it was just lurking on the end of our log, doing its best to look appetizing, leaving me free to watch what Blossom was doing at the far end of the beach.

BLOSSOM was a nice kid, two years and many ages younger than myself. He was desperately shy and had been dreading coming to the hut, torn between curiosity and his fear of the unknown.

He had been miserable for the first few days, but came out of his shell surprisingly quickly as soon as he was given a nickname. He was very proud of it, despite its connotations, and found that it allowed him the freedom to become someone else. Someone more outgoing, someone who belonged to a group that gave new names to one another.

He was still quiet, but very sensible and practical, quick to understand the sensitivities of others, and to move with a minimum of fuss to deal with real or imagined slights. He was a social asset, and a considerable artist. There were no books, no writing materi-als, no sketch pads in the hut. That was one of our understandings. We came here to be completely here, to focus on the present, not to live vicariously in some other time and place.

Those of us who loved to read experienced print-starvation, pouncing on those parts of our tidal flotsam that had any writing on them, relishing labels as though they were Mosaic tablets. But Blossom found a far more productive way of satisfying his cravings.

Most days, on an outgoing tide, he could be found somewhere on the beach, sketching with a stick in the wet sea sand. We usually left him alone at these times, but on several occasions when the tide was about to return and he was helping with the evening meal, I had sauntered over to where he had been working, and was astounded by what I found.

Almost without lifting his stick, he had created running friezes of figures, animal and human, exotic trees, unlikely buildings, futuristic vehicles, and old steam trains. Landscapes of the imagination, complete in every respect, rich in detail, impossible places that never existed for anyone else but him. And I would hang about there, enjoying his creations, reluctant to leave until it grew too dark to see or until the waves came back to reclaim their domain.

This morning Blossom's sketching was unusually intense. He was filling space as fast as the sea would let him, colonizing fresh surfaces as soon as they became available, losing some again to late waves. !Kamma couldn't contain his curiosity for long. He jumped up to get a closer look, and I followed on behind.

If Blossom was aware of our arrival, he showed no sign of it, and we walked slowly along the dry sand, looking at what he had done.

It was scary. Quite unlike anything else he had done before, and totally out of place on this brilliant day.

He had conjured up a nightmare scene. A dark underworld of wild-eyed monsters with dripping fangs. Beasts that glowered and grimaced in pain, both given and received. A pantheon of terrors, writhing across one another, slinking in and out of grottoes and groves, hell-bent on evil and unspeakable deeds. It was truly horrible, and made more so by being out here in the sun, flowing from the hand of a frightened child.

Blossom was white-faced and wincing, obviously hurting, terrified of what he was doing, and unable to stop—until !Kamma intervened.

He moved quickly to Blossom's side, put his own small brown right hand gently over Blossom's left, and slowed the manic movement down. It clearly wasn't easy. Whatever possessed the boy was reluctant to give ground, and they arm-wrestled for a while, until the tip of the stick stopped moving in mid-monster, leaving the last horror unfanged.

Nothing happened for a long while, and then Blossom's dead eyes slowly cleared, he stopped grinding his teeth, his face relaxed, and he looked up at !Kamma with recognition and relief. !Kamma smiled reassuringly, and suddenly the stick began to move again.

This time with an easy, flowing rhythm in an almost straight line, taking Blossom and !Kamma together in lockstep over to a new, virgin area of wet strand. And there, after a short pause, they began a delicate dance that left a very different kind of design in their train.

No monsters now, just elephants. A wonderful herd of elephants, small and large, their trunks swinging easily from side to side, heads dipping with every step, ears flapping like butterfly wings as they moved in single file, testing and tasting the ground as they traveled, without haste, just doing what elephants should.

They were beautiful uncomplicated elephants, their dignity and decency captured in a few flowing lines. Pure Blossom, with nothing nasty in it, just a herd moving silently from left to right, keeping appointments in far-flung places, as elephants will.

Blossom stopped, looked down at what they were doing, and smiled, gratefully. This was all right. He took his hand off the stick and gave !Kamma a little salute. Thank you!

!Kamma lifted his head in a dismissive gesture; it was nothing. . . .

But that was patently untrue. By this time, Owl and Starbuck and several of the others had joined us and were looking in wonder at the images, no one daring to step on them or say anything at all.

!Kamma was the first to respond. He acted alone now, holding the drawing stick out in front of him and moving along to his left, back to the straight line separating the demons from the elephants, where he began to make his own mark. An animal emerged, large, facing left, meeting the unnatural monsters head-on, holding the bridge, defending the herd with tusks long and straight. The style now was different, his rather than Blossom's, more of a caricature, but it was unquestionably our big white elephant.

Blossom blinked at it and said: "I need to go and lie down for a while." Owl went with him to the hut, and !Kamma nodded to himself and said: "*!Nau.*"

I DIDN'T know what to say.

It seemed clear to me that Blossom hadn't been himself. For a while there, he was definitely someone or something else, something unpleasant. This was a long time before *The Exorcist*, and nobody I knew had any experience with demonic possession. I had seen people in trance when I was a child in the north, but on the beach that day, I wasn't sure what to make of Blossom's behavior.

The only thing I could be sure of was that he had acted strangely and stopped doing that only when !Kamma took him in hand. It all seemed to have something to do with elephants in general and with the old white elephant in particular, so I looked carefully at the sketch that !Kamma had made.

Starbuck joined me there and said: "*!Nau.*"

I glared at him. "Not you too!"

"I don't think it's a name," he offered. "Not for that old bull, or any other elephant. I think it's a warning."

I looked at him carefully. He was serious. "Why?"

He shrugged. "I don't know, but every time !Kamma has used that word, his voice has changed. He sounds as though he is a little afraid, but also proud and respectful. As though he is talking about God."

He was right. !Kamma treated the white elephant as though it was both sacred and dangerous. He was very careful with it, regarding it with wonder and pleasure, but also with a measure of concern. Like a long-lost child that had suddenly reappeared, fully grown, with gifts of unknown things, powers as yet untested and undescribed.

I turned to !Kamma and, indicating his sketch, asked, *"!Nau?"* He nodded. Yes.

I pointed at the other elephants, and asked; *"!Nau?"* He shook his head, emphatically. No!

There was clearly a difference. We could all see and feel that, but it was hard to define.

!Kamma thought about it for a moment and then held up his hand. Look here! We did.

He pointed at the drawing he had made, indicating that it faced left, toward the demonic figures, which continued to exert menace, even in the bright sunlight. Then !Kamma took the drawing stick, retraced the line between the old bull and the nasties, and, with a flourish, wiped a whole intimidation of monsters out of existence.

He looked at us expectantly and, when we still didn't seem to understand, he rapidly sketched in another figure of the great white elephant right where the demons had been. And rushing ahead, this time with a large piece of driftwood in both hands, he erased every single ugly image on the beach.

When he turned around at the far end and came walking triumphantly back, we gave him a round of applause. He waved a hand impatiently at us—No, not me!—and, pointing down at the two sketches of the old bull, signed, "Him!" It was him, the great white elephant!

I stared down at the double depictions of the old bull. They were similar, but not the same . . . and suddenly I understood. This was not just an elephant. It was something in transition. Something both heroic and potentially harmful. Something that needed to be handled very carefully. It was alone, as many old bulls often are, because they can be difficult and dangerous. But no herd was complete without a patriarch, whose presence filtered down through the community, holding it together as royal chemicals empower a hive.

Too much too quickly had overwhelmed Blossom, the most sensitive of us, leaving him vulnerable to the collective demons that haunt us all. The white elephant was both the immediate cause and the ultimate cure. He was something we needed, but also needed to treat with caution, with the timeless rituals and ceremonies necessary to deal with fear. By playing at Strandlopers we had invited such experience in, long before we were ready to deal with the dangers that accompany rebirth and renewal.

We had been playing with fire, and were lucky to be only slightly singed!

THERE is, in southern Arizona on the border of Mexico, an unusual Amerindian tribe, the Papago, the "Bean People." They exist still: stately women in long dresses and big men with the kind of easy grace found only amongst those who don't have to fight to prove how strong they are.

They have always lived as nomads within sight of the sacred mountain Babaquivari, leaving it only to make pilgrimages across the Sonoran Desert down to the Sea of Cortez to bring back ceremonial salt. Unlike their neighbors the Navajo, Apache, and Seminole, they played no part in the western frontier wars against settlers and cavalry, and as a result they lost out when it came to treaties and reservations in the postwar period. To the new U.S. government, they were cowards of no account.

The Papago see it differently. For them, killing is a serious matter. They will fight, and have done so many times when directly threatened by Yaqui renegades, but steadfastly refuse to accept any macho notions of the "glory" of war. There are no conquering heroes in their history, no celebrations for victorious warriors returning from the fray. On the contrary, anyone who has blood on his hands is regarded as too "hot" to handle, a danger to Papago society.

No matter how justifiable or necessary the killing may have been, anyone involved is held at arm's length, obliged to remain out in the desert for weeks. And kept there in seclusion, tended by old people, those without fear, who know the rites, the fasts, and the sacramental ceremonies necessary to "cool" the killer down. Only then, when he has renounced his old life and been reborn, can he be reintroduced to his grateful community.

!Nau seems to be such a condition. A rite of transition. The dangerous state of being neither one thing or another. A time of expiation and submission, a search for purity.

Such notions make sense to me now. And I believe that even at the age of twelve, I was able to appreciate the essence of transition. As preteens we were intimately involved in such an experience. Starbuck called it "*!Nau* and Then." But I couldn't work out what it had to do with elephants.

!Kamma could have explained it if we had had a language in common. Years later, I had a chance to enjoy a long and spirited conversation with a !Kung "Bushman" of pure San stock. He manned a small desert plant nursery on the banks of the Orange River, specializing in what Afrikaans speakers call *vetplante*, literally "fat plants" or succulents. He had no English or Afrikaans, I had no San. The little Khoi I could remember from our time with !Kamma meant nothing on the edge of the Kalahari, but when it came to the taxonomy and description of plants in his care, we had Latin in common! How he learned his is a mystery, probably from a botanical missionary, but we had a very pleasant exchange which ended in my buying a boxful of specimens, all carefully classified. He apologized about a single unidentified aloe, however, explaining that he "knew its surname, but not its Christian name."

Names are important. They are not just convenient labels, but have a weight and history of their own. Knowing the name of something gives one power over it, which is why many tribal people use nicknames or "ekenames," added ones without pedigree, reserving their real names, the family names, for personal use.

And now that Starbuck and I had made some progress with the meaning of *!Nau*, we began to wonder about *!Kamma*.

Was that really his name, or was it too something more? Could it also be a description of his state? Was he also in transition . . . a bridge between the centuries?

It was enough to make our heads spin, so we put it on hold and went with him back to the hut for lunch.

WE spent a very pleasant afternoon.

!Kamma taught us how to make fire by friction, we taught him baseball.

He dug up an ant nest at the clifftop, showing us how to find the storehouse, a chamber filled with enough grass seed to make several meals. We showed him how to make a cat's cradle with string. He liked that.

!Kamma made a flute from a *matjie* reed and played a sad tune on it. We sang him a few rousing verses of "Onward Christian Soldiers." It sounds silly now, but before the pop explosion and independent radio stations, our musical currency in the old South Africa was largely confined to *Hymns Ancient and Modern*.

The Rock did catch a *leervis*, a large one, and we barbecued it with herbs !Kamma picked on the hill, sitting in an arc in front of the fire, looking across it to the ocean, with !Kamma in the center of us. All twelve of us, arrayed in a totally unconscious parody of the Last Supper.

It was just that.

At the precise moment the sun went down to our right, the full moon burst over the horizon to our left in full glowing reflection, looking far larger than it ever does overhead. Solid silver in the clean ocean air. And as it pulled itself clear of the horizon, !Kamma leapt to his feet and shouted *"Khab!"* and raised both arms in welcome.

As one, we did the same, hailing the moon as he had—*"Khab!"* And we followed him, step by step, as he began a stately dance, stamping his feet, looking down left and right as each foot fell, clapping his hands to the rhythm.

We moved in single file, line dancing, swaying to the beat, marking out a circle in the sand around the fire, pausing every time he did, raising our arms and shouting, *"Khab!* Praise the moon!" For it was obvious what all this was about.

THE moon is not to be laughed at.

In Khoisan folklore, the moon is alive and never dies. It grows large and disappears, but is always born again, coming back small in a matter of days. Unlike the sun, which never changes and is unapproachable, we can talk to the moon and ask for anything. Children, rain, luck in the hunt. And the moon answers, sending a moth in reply, carrying good news if it comes to the fire. But don't mention the hare!

Once, it is said, the moon had an important message to send to the people. The news that we, like the moon itself, would never die, but rise again. Such tidings were too important to entrust to a moth, so the moon ordered a fleet hare to carry the message. He did, but having such a short attention span, he got it all turned about in his head. He said that people who died would never rise again. They were completely finished, forever.

And so was the hare. When the moon discovered his mistake, it heated a stone in the fire of the sun, held the hare down, and burnt his mouth, leaving a permanent scar and a split in his upper lip. And condemned it to dance madly whenever the moon was full in the sky.

Which is why those who know also greet the full moon, making it welcome, shouting praise for blessings granted, dancing well in the hope that it might send the good news again, in safer hands. A porcupine perhaps?

So we danced.

We danced until the moon was a full hand above the horizon and had shrunk to its usual size. Then we sat once more around the fire, not speaking, just looking into the embers, thinking our own thoughts and happy to be where we were.

Having !Kamma in our midst had changed many things. Before he arrived, we were Strandlopers only in name. We had adopted the lifestyle and become pretty good at fending for ourselves. We had learned a great deal, but something was always missing. Something we recognized now as spirit. We had played at beachwalking and enjoyed doing so, but not until he came into our lives did we under-stand that this was not enough. We had the style, but not the life.

In the days B.K., Before !Kamma, we just came and went, tak-ing summer holidays in Stone Age style. Now A.K., we knew better. This was more than just a game. This thing we did one month a year was something that others, like !Kamma, had done as a way of life for millennia. We had always known this, but never taken it to heart, never given it the full respect it deserved as a culture. One that probably played a large and seminal part in our own history, not only in the Cape, but everywhere our ancestors had grown into con-scious beings as a direct result of living well, eating the right things, having fresh water, a mild climate, and the time to sit on the shore of a great ocean, out of the cut and thrust of competition elsewhere, growing big brains and reaching human fulfillment.

It was never that cerebral, of course. Not at the time, but we sensed even then that the moon was indeed still in the business of sending messages.

What !Kamma got we will never know, but it must have been the Khoi equivalent of "Phone home," because we never saw him again. When we stumbled off to sleep, he was still sitting in front of the fire, humming gently to himself. When we awoke, he was gone.

THERE was not a trace of him anywhere.

The tide had washed the beach clean, and an unseasonal shower during the night had obliterated all our tracks in the dunes and around the hut. He brought nothing with him, left nothing behind. The others got up, washed, went about their usual business. It was as if the last few days had never existed.

No one brought a wristwatch to the hut. To mark the passage of time, we preferred to cut notches into a piece of driftwood that hung on the side wall. Each morning one of us, the Rock this summer, cut the notch and blocked off each seven days, reminding us when four weeks had passed and we had to hike back and meet our transport at the old farmhouse.

There were five days to go, and I tried to remember how many days had passed since !Kamma materialized. I couldn't remember, and no one else seemed to know. Had it all happened? Was he real? What was in the herbs he had collected as his contriubution to our meals?

I asked Owl, who was usually an early bird, if he had seen !Kamma. He shook his head. I stopped the Rock and said, "Have you seen any Hottentots this morning?" He looked at me as if I was mad, and hurried past. I was beginning to worry. Was I going crazy, had I dreamed it all?

Then Starbuck came over. "Ho *suri!*" he said. And I let out a long breath of relief. The kid had bullied !Kamma into teaching him Khoi and paid more attention than the rest of us, but that was one word I had picked up too. It means "chief" and is a sort of honorary title adopted by a people who have no real chiefs.

"Thank God," I said. "I was beginning to think that I had imagined the last three days."

"No. Not all of it, anyway," he said slowly. "But you're right. There are parts of it I have trouble with too. Where is he?"

"I think he has gone. Permanently."

Starbuck thought this through, and nodded. "Yes, that seems right."

He kept amazing me with his cool acceptance of the world and his insights about it.

"Where do you think he has gone?" I asked.

"Oh, he goes back," said Starbuck. "Until next time."

He made !Kamma sound like one of those little figures in a cuckoo clock, popping in and out on cue. But that wasn't a bad description of our experience of him. He was there right after we first saw the great white elephant. And I realized I wasn't surprised that !Kamma had gone, because for the first time in three days I no longer felt that trembling in the air, that "certain warmth" that comes with the knowledge of elephant nearby. It had echoed quietly in me since the day at the gorge, but now it was gone, and so was he.

Were they one and the same?

THAT couldn't be the end of it! I let it go for a while and then cornered Owl and Starbuck together, feeding their captive crickets on breakfast scraps.

"Feel like a hike?" I asked.

They didn't look very keen and waited for more information.

"I want to go back to the gorge. I want to climb across to the other side and take a look around there."

Owl turned to Starbuck and asked: "What is grayish and has four legs and a trunk?"

Starbuck replied brightly: "An elephant."

"Aha," said Owl. "So what *isn't* gray, and has no legs and no trunk?"

They turned to me in unison and cried: "No elephants!" And laughed so hard they almost lost their crickets.

"You two need to get out more," I said. "Meet me at the trail in two minutes."

We walked quickly along the cliffs, past Losklip, and looked across the gorge. The milkwood tree was still there, without elephant. We nevertheless worked our way along the cliff until we could plot a route across and started down.

It wasn't easy. The forest was almost impenetrable in parts, but we battered through with our sticks, refreshed ourselves in the stream at the bottom, and began the long climb back up the far side. Hyraxes scattered in our path, raising their rump hairs in protest. We saw an eagle swoop by in search of sleepy *dassies*, avoided a large puffadder lying wonderfully camouflaged in leaf litter, and eventually reached the top, scrambling out very close to the big tree.

When we had got our breaths back, we went to stand right beneath the tree, where the great elephant had been, looking out to sea. The view was spectacular. The cliff dropped eight hundred feet straight down into the ocean. The sound of waves breaking on the rocks below was loud and clear, and the shade of the leathery leaves very welcome.

The sandstone under our bare feet was flat, smooth, and weatherworn. It felt good, but we left no prints on it, and neither had the elephant. We looked for signs of browsing along the gnarled and twisted trunk, but no one likes milkwood much. It has a milky latex.

We searched nearby for fresh droppings, but found none. We walked back into the forest and picked up a trail, but no recent signs of elephant. And in the end, we had to admit defeat. We were no nearer learning anything new about our elephant.

Before setting off back to the hut, I stood once more where the old bull had been and closed my eyes, searching for something, a scent perhaps, anything that would add substance to his existence. And when I opened my eyes and looked down, there it was!

Scratched into the smooth slate of sandstone was a delicate design. A compact, controlled, and graceful composition consisting of loops and spikes, starting at the top and sweeping down in graceful arcs, left and right, but always returning to a cluster at the top. As though the entire tracing had been done in one sitting, without once breaking the line.

And lying a trunk length away was a quartz pebble with an abraded tip. Just right for doodling.

IN 1982, Jerome Witkin, a professor in the Department of Art Education at Syracuse University in New York, was asked to evaluate some abstract drawings done by a fourteen-year-old called Siri. He liked them and described the work as "very lyrical, very beautiful—positive, affirmative and tense—lovely!"

Hope Irvine, chairman of the department, agreed. She said the work was definitely more than random scribbling and looked like "the more sophisticated thing that adults do when they try to draw like children." And Howard Gardner, a local art critic and author, saw "definite development" between earlier and later examples of the young artist's work.

All of which was music to the ears of David Gucwa at the Burnet Park Zoo, because Siri was an Asian elephant who had produced the engravings spontaneously by scratching them into a concrete floor with a pebble held in her one-fingered trunk.

Siri started something. Given the chance, Beulah at the New York State Fair, Lulu at the Buffalo Zoo, and several elephants at the Washington Park Zoo in Oregon, all produced work of their own. Work over which the well-known Dutch expressionist Willem de Kooning enthused. And soon more than twenty other pachyderm painters all over the world were hard at work on their own compositions. Some even sold well.

Siri was not the first artistic nonhuman. In the 1960s, Desmond Morris persuaded Congo, a male chimpanzee at the London Zoo, to begin a series of crayon and poster-paint works, each carrying a characteristic fan-shaped "signature." He was followed by Baltimore Betsy, a female chimp in Maryland, and by Maharani Indira, an elephant at Ontario Zoological Park, in the 1970s. But all these animal artists drew and painted only after being prompted by a human who supplied them with all the necessary materials.

Siri was caught in the wild in Thailand at the age of two and never encouraged to paint or draw in any way. She seems to have discovered art all on her own, apparently for amusement, working at night in her lonely enclosure.

If the impulse to do so is so strong, it suggests that the origins of artistic endeavor may well be widespread and ought to be looked for in nature, most profitably perhaps amongst wild elephants.

In 1951, I knew nothing of this.

What we had found was a scribble, an artifact, something that was not produced by accident or erosion, and a pebble that appeared to be the instrument involved.

I picked it up and thought I caught a trace of something musky, but couldn't be sure. I traced one of the grooves in the engraving and it fit perfectly. We had the "smoking gun," but no suspect. I held the pebble tightly in my closed hand and something familiar chimed in my chest. A feeling I knew well and associated directly with the discovery of old stone tools.

Stone Age implements abound in Africa. There are places where the whole surface of the soil is carpeted with flakes and cores and hand axes. In parts of the Cape, you can pick up as many as you can carry, though this is discouraged by archaeologists. They are almond- or tear-shaped, as large as a man's hand, and chipped with considerable care on both sides into elegant symmetrical forms. I had found my first one at the age of seven in a washed-out gully and known, from the moment I first saw it, that this was more than just a stone. It was a message. I had knelt down and looked at it for a long time before I could bring myself to touch the smooth gold surface. But when I finally did, it was like an electric shock. I knew I was the first person to handle that stone since the ancient man who made it had left it there. And it seemed to me that our fingertips were touching across many thousands of years.

That pebble had something of the same feel, with different and interesting overtones. I slipped it into my pocket—and have it still.

THERE is nothing logical about a hand ax.

It is unnecessarily beautiful. The delicacy of its design, the quality of its workmanship, and the time and effort involved go far beyond functional demand. Why go to all this trouble? If what you need is a point or a sharp edge to help you skin an animal, a far cruder tool would have been just as effective. And yet the hand ax was universally popular, the Boy Scout knife of the ancient world. It occurs everywhere our ancestors lived, in Africa, Europe, and Asia over a period of more than a million years, laying the foundation for both technology and art. It was our first essay in style, the first real evidence of human creativity.

The origin of consciousness and self-awareness lies at the heart of debates about human uniqueness. And one of the few things on which everyone involved seems to agree is that our hands, our five-fingered, grasping extremities with opposable thumbs, have played a major part in the evolution of our new, big brains. It was these that made it possible for our ancestors to pick things up, to "manipulate" them, to hold them up for examination. And it was this ability that led, along with binocular vision, to a foreshortening of the face, and to a bipedal posture that freed the hands completely for even closer scrutiny of the world around us.

Good hands, of course, are not uniquely human. Most of our primate relatives have similar advantages. As do raccoons and coatimundis and many rodents, each benefiting in different degrees from having five, four, or even three versatile fingers. But most discussions about such adaptations tend to ignore the fact that there is another line of evolution which has taken an entirely different direction involving just two fingers, not on the end of an arm, but on the front of a face.

A case not of manipulation, but "trombipulation."

ELEPHANT trunks are unique. If we knew proboscideans from fossils alone, it is highly unlikely that our reconstructions of them would include the huge "face-finger." Any palaeontologist brave enough to extrapolate such an outlandish device would have been asked to take a drug test.

We know now, of course, that the trunk is an elongated fusion of the nose and the upper lip, involving a totally novel adaptation of the nasal muscles. Explanations for how it happened remain so convoluted that it is tempting to ignore the lot and resort instead

to Kipling's crocodile on "the great grey-green, greasy Limpopo."
But, broadly, the answer seems to lie in the problem of growing
big and finding it increasingly difficult to reach the ground or
drink. The giraffe solution was a longer neck, the elephant's a
new nose.

Most mammals have a set of six major muscles in their snouts.
Elephants now have over 100,000 muscles, endlessly subdivided
and arranged in superficial longitudinal and deeper transverse
bands. How they manage to carry out all the contortions of which a
trunk seems capable remains mysterious. The answer may be a
closed hydraulic system, operated by the muscles, pumping fluid
into different areas as necessary, but there are no obvious
fluid-filled spaces in the trunk.

In many ways, a trunk is even more versatile than the human
hand. It is powerful, capable of lifting weights exceeding a thousand
pounds; and it is precise, picking up objects just one tenth of an
inch in diameter and discriminating between them. Elephants use it
for eating, drinking, dusting, sparring, fighting, throwing, playing,
spraying, scratching, sniffing, smelling, trumpeting, caressing, communicating with others, and reassuring the young.

It is one of the most expressive organs in the entire animal
kingdom.

The most sensitive part of the trunk is at the ever-moving tip,
which is adorned by two projecting fingers. This is the African elephant's "hand," with which it can and does make and use tools,
picking up palm fronds to use as flyswatters, or collecting and
preparing twigs small enough to remove ticks from between folds in
the skin.

Altogether, this "fifth limb" separates elephants from every
other hoofed animal, giving them the sort of dexterity that is more
characteristic of monkeys and apes. And this capacity for maneuver
and manipulation seems to have made changes in the elephant's
brain, making it complex in ways that mirror our own complexity.

In most mammals, young are born with brains of almost adult size, growing very little after birth. Wildebeests, for instance, know most of what they need to know right from the start. More intelligent species depend on a period of learning and greater brain development as they grow. Rhinoceroses are born with brains 90 percent of the adult size. Our nearest relative, the chimpanzee, gives birth to babies with 54 percent of their adult brain weight. But the Elephant's Child, "full of satiable curiosity," is born with just 35 percent of its brain size and potential, adding the rest in a period of dependency and social education which is far longer, more like our own. In humans, the brain at birth is 29 percent of its adult size and weight. And in both elephants and humans this extra tissue is added to the cerebrum and cerebellum, where memory and awareness, and perhaps creativity, can be located.

Genetically, we are poles apart, but in habit and concern, humans and elephants seem to meet in many ways on strangely common ground.

OWL and Starbuck were very frisky on the way back, racing each other across the gorge. They were soon out of my sight, but I could still hear snatches of their conversation.

"Why are elephants wrinkled?"

"Did you ever try to iron one?"

I suspected that these high spirits owed much to our failure to find an elephant that day, but elephants were still very much on my mind too. They seem to have the ability to linger on in a landscape long after they have gone. Some sort of elephant aftermath, like a vapor trail or persistent shadow, a presence that is embedded in the soil itself and seeps out as you tread on ancient paths.

When I got to the clifftop on the other side of the gorge, I stopped for a while and looked back at the milkwood tree. No sign of an elephant, but the image of the big pale bull was still sharp in my memory, and I could almost see him again, looking out to sea, deep in thought, exercising his big brain as it idled. Letting the tip of his trunk swing as it followed his thoughts, magnifying them as a pantograph can, inscribing them permanently on a tablet of stone with the aid of a convenient quartz pebble.

I fingered the pebble in my pocket and made myself a promise. I would come back one day and find out more about the Knysna elephants. Learn everything there was to know about their history and their prospects. There were only a few days left of our Strandloper life for this year, but I had one more chance to return to the hut the following summer. After that I would be fourteen and would have to get serious about matriculating, getting into university, and finding a career. I had been leaning toward medicine, but that didn't feel quite right anymore. I needed more than one species in my life. I wanted elephants. . . .

My reverie was interrupted by raucous voices: "Oi! Are you coming? It's getting late and Rock promised lobster for dinner!"

So he had. I turned away from the gorge and chased after the others, enjoying the feel of the sun on my back and the sound of their laughter up ahead.

We were okay. We were the Strandlopers!

The
Iron
Age

MALACHY lives alone in a stone cottage just outside a small village on the west coast of Ireland. He has never been married and keeps very much to himself, coming into his favorite bar each afternoon for just one pint of porter. On Sundays he attends Mass and lingers in the village just long enough to exchange greetings with a few friends who worry about him only if he fails to keep to his usual routine.

Malachy was born during the times of the Land Bill and the struggle for Irish Home Rule, no one is sure exactly when, but consensus in the village suggests that he must be well into his nineties. What can be seen of his skin is almost black, ingrained from sitting too close to the peat fire he keeps burning in the hearth through all the seasons. There is no indoor plumbing in his home, and when he nurses his drink in front of the bar fire in winter, his old tweed jacket steams like the pelt of a bear.

The District Health Inspector has considered committing him to hospital once a year, just to give him a good bath, but she cannot find sufficient medical grounds to do so. His health is remarkably good, and there is nothing to suggest that his mind is in any way impaired—except for the fact that he claims to see an elephant near his home.

Malachy lives on the shore of a rocky arm of Donegal Bay, facing south at the foot of a mountain covered in gorse and heather. And, when pressed, he insists that every evening, just after dusk, a large red hairy elephant with two great white curved tusks comes out of the eastern hills across the cove. It drinks in the stream that runs down to the shore and then makes its way silently up the lane outside his gate, padding and swaying into the high shadows behind him.

Nobody has ever seen this extraordinary animal, and there is talk about the homemade liquor called poteen, but every evening his old sheepdog runs down and barks at the cottage gate. And it just so happens that a few years ago, long after Malachy first started talking about his visitations, the remains of a male woolly mammoth, complete with tusks, were discovered in the bogs of Aghnadarragh, just across the border in County Down!

CHAPTER FOUR

Losing the Elephant

Man on this planet has reached the point where he
needs all the friendship he can find, and in his
loneliness he has need of all the elephants.
—ROMAIN GARY in *The Roots of Heaven*, 1958

ELEPHANTS are surprisingly difficult to count. Despite their size, they have an uncanny ability to dissolve into shadows, disappearing in plain sight, reappearing where you least expect them. Even from the air, it is hard to untangle a herd, breaking down the flow, turning a tide of great gray backs into numbers. And whenever you can, the arithmetic is dismal.

At the turn of the nineteenth century, there were perhaps 200,000 elephants in the wild in Asia. Today there are fewer than fifty thousand. Ten million African elephants roamed the savannas of Africa in Hemingway's day. Now there may be no more than half a million. It is a losing battle. Elephants everywhere are dying faster than they can reproduce.

On average, elephants can expect to live to about sixty-five, at which age they run out of teeth and starve. Females reach puberty, just as we do, at about twelve years old and remain fertile until fifty. Every gestation occupies almost two years, but the calving interval in most of Africa is nearer five years, which means that the annual population growth rate, even under ideal conditions, is seldom more than 4 percent.

Elephants are the slowest breeders in the animal kingdom, but left to their own devices, even they are theoretically capable of turning one breeding pair into fifteen million questing trunks in just five hundred years. This hasn't happened, of course. Elephant numbers in Africa were controlled historically by climatic factors such as periodic droughts, but an even more important influence during the last century has been direct competition between elephants and humans for the same resources.

Elephants have always loomed large in Africa. Right through the course of human history, there seems to have been a sense of shared destiny, even respect, in some areas compounded by the recognition of spirits of tribal ancestors in individual living elephants. Folklore in several parts of West Africa even traces the origin of domestic crops to special seeds wrapped in neat gift packages of elephant dung. Before agriculture, nomadic pastoralists and elephants cooperated in the sense that elephants converted woodland to grassland, while herds of domestic cattle on the resulting savanna stimulated a regrowth of the kind of bush elephants prefer. But ever since cultivation, this symbiosis has broken down. Every acre under crops is one lost to elephants, and each area set aside for conservation inhibits the expansion of human populations in the same way. The result is competitive exclusion.

In East Africa in 1925, elephants ranged across 87 percent of the land, providing substance to Jonathan Swift's observation that the geographers of his day were forced to fill great gaps on their maps with "elephants for want of towns." People in that time farmed islands in a sea of elephants. But by 1975, elephants had become confined to just 27 percent of the land, their place taken by farmers working ever smaller family plots. Poaching for ivory has certainly taken its toll, but the "elephant problem," which obsessed colonial governments to the extent that killing them became the primary function of so-called game departments, has been replaced by a "people problem." Elephants now survive on shrinking islands in a sea of people.

This rise in human population reflects the decline in elephant numbers so precisely that it has become possible even to predict the latter's imminent extinction. In Kenya, elephants are in danger of disappearing forever when human population density reaches 215 per square mile. In less productive Zimbabwe, elephant Armageddon looms when any more than fifty humans come to live in each square mile. The deadline will be reached in Kenya any moment now, but Zimbabwe has already passed its sell-by date. Somewhere between these two extremes of abundance and alarm, during the mid-1950s, I graduated from school at the age of just fifteen. Skipping a year early in the process meant that I was always younger than my classmates, and far too immature to tackle the pressure cooker of university life. My parents still hoped for a doctor in the family, but frequent exposure to hospital routines during my more accident-prone years had left me with mixed feelings about medical science. So I begged for a year out and time to make up my mind.

I got it.

In the rest of Africa, the march to freedom had begun. Patrice Lumumba was already exercising his intelligence and energy in the struggle for black equality with white Belgians in the Congo. Jomo Kenyatta was planning Kenya's future from a British jail, and Kwame Nkrumah had to be let out from *his* prison cell to form the first black government on the Gold Coast. There was talk everywhere of "Africanness," but in the south, concentration was still largely on Afrikaners.

Here a white minority government that believed it had a mandate from God was strengthening its control with legislations that suspended civil liberties, prohibited interracial marriages, restricted educational opportunities, and segregated the country along racial lines. In South Africa, 87 percent of the land was populated not by elephants, but by white people, who succeeded as early as 1910 in becoming the first nation in Africa to achieve independence from colonial rule. Freedom for black South Africans had to wait another eighty-four years.

As a fifteen-year-old white boy, I was only dimly aware of all this turmoil. My rights were being eroded too, but not in any way that restricted my freedom to go where I pleased. So I went in search of something that had been much on my mind for several years. I went looking again for wild elephants!

SOUTH AFRICA has an inordinate fondness for fences.

Its half a million square miles is crisscrossed with an elaborate network of barbed wire strung along farm boundaries or marking internal pastures in patterns designed to deter casual trespassers, keep stock from straying, and defend livestock from marauding jackals.

Driving cross-country was once an adventure measured in gates, many manned by juvenile tollkeepers with big smiles who would open and close the rusty barriers for a penny. The arrival of real traffic led later to endless miles of paved highway protected on either side by very long, straight fence lines relieved only by occasional shrikes or buzzards doing sentry duty on convenient perches. All very tidy and territorial—except where elephants were concerned.

South Africa was colonized by men with good European guns who, from the very outset in the sixteenth century, never hesitated to use them. The last elephant in Cape Town was killed in 1652, and by 1761 there were none anywhere inside the Olifants River that marks the elephant-free northern boundary of the Cape Floral Kingdom. In 1830, a long-overdue prohibition was placed on all elephant killing in the Cape Colony, but the damage was already done,

and unruly hunters simply took their trade further north. By the end
of the nineteenth century, all elephants had been removed entirely
from anywhere in South Africa, except for a few small inhospitable
retreats. One of which, I had heard, was about to be given the ultimate accolade, South Africa's most coveted and conspicuous measure of real worth. It was going to be *fenced,* bringing an end to one
of the least savory events in African conservation.

Even then, I sensed that this event was pivotal, one of those
moments that later would be seen to be a turning point in the history
of our relationship with the rest of nature. A time when, faced with the
growing loneliness of careless extinctions, we took thought and actually did the right thing. And I wanted to be a part, however peripheral,
of that moment. So I went to a place known simply as the Addo. . . .

EUROPEAN hunters were not the first to kill African elephants for
something other than their meat. From about the ninth century,
Arab traders worked their way down the east coast bringing metals
and ceramics to markets where they exchanged these goods for
coconut oil, turtle shell, skins, and ivory. The people with whom they
traded were known collectively as the Zanj, today's Swahili speakers,
who in turn did business in the interior. Early engravings of the ivory
trade show lines of docile elephants falling obligingly into pit traps
armed with sharp stakes. Something of the sort probably happened,
but introduced weapons and a burgeoning local Iron Age soon made
killing more efficient and predictable, adding a new factor to the
equations of competitive exclusion. And before long, elephants gave
way and withdrew into more difficult, less disputed territories.

The Addo is one of these. A wilderness near the Sundays River,
where the folded mountains of the southern Cape run out into the
sea, channeling all traffic into a natural elephant trap at the eastern

limit of the *fynbos* habitat. Four rocky chains of hills from the interior converge there on an alluvial plain of bright red soil bound together by an almost impenetrable thicket of just one succulent plant.

Portulacaria afra is a hardy, drought-resistant species with round fleshy leaves and small, starlike flowers, purple-pink in color. It grows, coincidently, to the height of an elephant and is known locally as *spekboom*—"bacon tree," from its waxy appearance—or *olifantskos*—the "food of the elephant." They were made for each other.

There is little surface water in the Addo, but the nearby Sundays River provides irrigation for agriculture, and therein lies the problem. In 1820, the British government settled veterans of the Napoleonic Wars on Algoa Bay, a windy strand previously known only as the turning point for the first voyage round the Cape by Portuguese explorer Bartholomeu Dias in 1488. Now five thousand men, women, and children, the first British farmers in South Africa, found themselves marooned on a wild frontier, caught in a pincer movement between white Boers and black Xhosa deeply involved in territorial disputes over cattle. These were resolved at great cost by the first "Kafir War" of 1834, but even when that ended, settlers had to deal with marauding elephants venturing out of the Addo to supplement their monotonous diet of *Portulacaria* with everything cultivated in British fields and gardens.

The result was inevitable—more skirmishes which continued unabated for an entire century, coming to a head only in 1920 with the introduction by the farmers of a hired gun in the form of saturnine elephant killer Major Philip Jacobus "Jungle Man" Pretorius.

I LEARNED about Pretorius from John Pringle, a descendant of one of the original settler families, who farmed in the foothills near the Addo.

It was still safe to hitchhike in those days, and John picked me up near Grahamstown University, responding, I liked to think, to my

irresistible wayside "child of distressed gentlefolk" routine. Or perhaps just because he wanted company.

He turned out to be very good company indeed. A well-read
man, silver-haired and somewhere in his seventies, but still curious
and finding enlightenment and entertainment in the doings of the
world around him.

"Ja," he said. "I remember Pretorius. He was a funny bugger.
Took himself very seriously. Never saw him smile, but then I suppose there wasn't much fun in what he did. He lived dangerously!

"He looked like an Arab. Thin, dark, and watchful, with that gray-
ness deep in his skin that comes from too many bouts of malaria. He
started early, serving as a transport rider for the British South African
Company in Rhodesia in 1899, when he was still only sixteen!"

My age, I thought, with a twinge of envy.

"I never liked him much," said John, "but General Jannie Smuts
trusted Pretorius enough to make him Chief Scout in the East African
Campaign of World War One. He apparently roamed about behind
enemy lines, collecting information, risking his life every day. It was he
who discovered the hiding place of the German cruiser *Königsberg*—
the one that sank HMS *Pegasus* in Zanzibar and took refuge in the
Rufiji Delta. There is no doubting his courage, but I did question the
man's morals. He killed too many animals for my liking. It was only
through a gun that he ever expressed himself completely. . . ."

John invited me to stay at his farm while I went about my business of getting a close look at the elephants of the Addo, and in the
course of many pleasant evenings on his deep veranda I learned
about the Jungle Man's ignoble task in that part of the Cape.

"He was invited here," said John, "by the bloody Administrator
himself. A purely political issue. Just to keep the Moaning Minnies
amongst the settlers happy. There were over a hundred elephants in
the Addo then, already a much-reduced herd, safe in the succulent
forest. The largest population in South Africa at that time. Sure, they
raided the nearest farms and plundered crops and vegetable gardens

in the dark, but every one of those most affected—some of them good friends of mine—had pushed too far into the Addo, taking over elephant territory piece by piece. They were asking for trouble! And they kept forgetting that we were all given land here free, or at very low cost, precisely *because* there were elephants in the region!"

John never used the term "competitive exclusion," but he understood exactly what it meant and how it worked. "It's a matter of give and take," he declared, "and my sympathies lie with the *ellies*. I suppose something had to be done, but none of us expected the Angel of Death!"

THE hunt, tracking down sources of high-protein food and making it available to ourselves and our close associates, is as old as human history. Hunting, on the other hand, is a recent and quite different development. It is one of the refinements of our species, one of the prices we have had to pay for so-called sophistication.

Hunts, particularly those involving the killing of dangerous or competitive animals, are the stuff of folklore. As hunter-gatherers, we grew up around campfires where tales were told of danger and defiance, of courage and cunning, stories that nearly always revealed as much about the hunters as they did about the hunted. The mystique of the hunt is powerful and deeply embedded in our blood. It had to be. It was part of our strategy for survival in a hostile world for millions of years, and natural selection favored those of us who were best at it.

The instinct to track and secure still rules our lives, even if it appears now only in the mask of wildlife photography or aggressive business tactics. The thrill is in the hunt itself, rather than the kill, and it is easy to justify and condone what is done in the name of sportmanship, of playing the "game." The very use of that word for both the process and the prey is revealing. It draws attention to the fact that hunting is now more than a matter of finding food. It has become a recreation (another interesting word) of the real thing. Something done by gentlemen for their own satisfaction, but still an enterprise that produces a very potent rush of adrenaline.

Theodore Roosevelt went further, giving hunting a political dimension: "The chase is among the best of all national pastimes; it cultivates rugged and stalwart democracy and that vigorous manliness for the lack of which in a nation, as in an individual, the possession of no other qualities can possibly atone."

Fine words, but difficult to square with the practice of many "gentlemen" when confronted, away from home, with the abundance of "game" in colonial Africa. Following David Livingstone's first expedition into the interior in the 1850s, a great rush of European and American hunting men poured into "the Territory" (now Zambia), killing every elephant in sight. Hundreds of thousands died there for no good reason; a further 585,000 were wiped out in the Congo in the next half century; and the massacre continued, bringing down at least another million elephants in both West and East Africa when settlers and farmers moved in between 1860 and 1910.

Much of this was wanton slaughter, brought about by greed on the part of adventurers and fortune hunters, but even the naturalists among them were far from blameless. The best of these, Frederick Courteney Selous, added substantially to knowledge about the Rhodesias and East Africa, collecting natural history specimens and ethnological information, which he published in several books. But he also hunted freely, for profit and fun, killing more elephants than he could ever remember.

Selous died as he would have wished, in battle for his country, killed by a sniper in 1917 while guiding a column of British troops into German-held Tanganyika. A mission he accepted at short notice when the regular scout received new orders and went instead to lead the Cape Corps to Rufiji and the destruction of the

Königsberg. The man that Selous, and a large number of elephants, died for was none other than the infamous Major Pretorius!

TWO years after the war ended, Pretorius was contacted by a fellow officer, Major Sillick, then a member of the town council of Uitenhage, which owned and leased valuable land around the Addo. At first he refused the assignment, but when the Addo was described to him as a "death trap" and he learned that even his hero Selous had turned down the job because "no one could hunt those elephants out," he changed his mind.

"It was pride," said John Pringle. "That and a .475 Jeffries double-barreled rifle, all expenses and the ivory as well. Even so, it wasn't easy. No one would go into the Addo with him. The place had a hoodoo on it. The only help he could secure were condemned men awaiting their death sentence in Uitenhage Jail.

"The man had nerves of iron. You had to grant him that, but there was something creepy about his whole approach. He was not a hunter. He was an executioner. The bugger even had himself a killing suit, made entirely of black leather—boots, pants, and a high-necked jacket with pockets for shells. Dressed to kill, with his hair parted right down the middle, he looked like something from another planet. Something truly sinister. Though I have to say that most of the undergrowth beneath the bacon trees consists of what we call *num-nums*, diabolically spiny bushes that belong to the same lethal family as African arrow poisons. Leather may be exactly what one needs!"

When I asked John what history would make of Major Pretorius, he thought a long while and said: "The man waged war against the Addo herd. That was what he was employed to do, to wipe them out forever. What worried me most was that he enjoyed his job too much. He also enjoyed an audience, doing bloody silly things like deliberately breaking an elephant's spine with his first shot, before running up its broad back to dispatch it with a second shot in the brain. Then he and his "secretary," Agnus Godfrey, she clothed in all the latest fashions, would sit on the corpse of the latest casualty, posing for the benefit of their own professional photographer!"

And when I wondered how many elephants Pretorius had killed in the Addo, John replied: "I don't know. Pretorius himself was never sure, though he had been asked to keep a record. Estimates range from one hundred to one hundred thirty. Nor do I know how many were left. Somewhere between eleven and sixteen is the consensus, all of which fled into the truly impregnable valleys of the Zuurberg."

He paused and sighed. "By the end of 1920, there were probably no more than one hundred twenty elephants left in all of South Africa, including the Addo survivors. Down from an estimated one hundred thousand in 1652. We all bear responsibility for this terrible record. With very few exceptions, the attitude of government and people to the fate of our elephants was one of general apathy.

"But a decade later, in 1931, seventeen thousand acres of the Addo was finally proclaimed the Addo Elephant National Park. That was great! The only problem was the elephants were somewhere else at the time and had to be driven into the park by its newly employed rangers. Twelve were eventually bullied into place, but getting them to stay there has been a huge problem, because the survivors of the Pretorius Massacre are an unruly bunch of elephants.

"They are wary and wily, declaring war themselves on humans at every opportunity, trampling down fences, pulling up water pipes, damaging dams, and even killing people—four at the latest count. We seem to have created the most dangerous elephants in the world!"

FOR years, the Addo's "Dirty Dozen" did as they pleased, causing havoc on the adjoining farms, finally earning their old reputation for being "rogues," "outlaws," and "ferocious thieves of the worst kind." After Pretorius, everything changed for the worse.

I was told the story of a farmer carrying a wagonload of oats to market, who found that he was being followed by several of the marauders. As they gained on him, he threw a bale of oats onto the roadway. This bought him some time, but before long the elephants were on his tail again, and another bale was sacrificed. There was very little of the farmer's load left when he finally emerged from elephant territory, but he had no doubt that giving up the crop had saved his life.

Others went instead for their guns, and several more wandering elephants died, raising the awful possibility that the new elephant park would be one without elephants at all. In 1934, Warden Harold Trollope began experimenting with electric fences, but the elephants soon discovered that dropping a log on the wires shorted out the circuit by grounding it, and that approach was abandoned. Ten years later, ranger Graham Armstrong came up with a better idea. He discovered that heavy steel ropes used to lift elevators and cable cars had to be replaced at regular intervals and were being scrapped, and that many cities in South Africa were tearing up their obsolete tram tracks. Tests using these secondhand materials as fences were run in the Kruger National Park, and in 1954, eight thousand acres of the Addo Park were surrounded by such a recycled barricade.

This is what I had come to see, just weeks after its completion. An earthen dike topped with an elephant-proof fence twelve miles long, circumscribing a large part of the Addo, like Africa's answer to the Great Wall of China. It was awesome. The only proper symbol of South Africa's new regard for its largest citizens. A super-surround for super-beings, finally housed in a place of their own.

I walked the entire perimeter one day with a ranger not much older than myself, hoping to see at least one of the last Cape herd testing its boundaries. There were plenty of tracks to show where elephants had patrolled all along the cleared area between the fence and the wall of succulent vegetation within, but no sight of the new inhabitants.

As we walked, the ranger talked about his charges. "These elephants are nothing like those old hands in the Kruger Park. Most of them haven't been shot at recently, but they have long memories and remain very cautious. They move around mainly after dark and respond very aggressively to any human approaches. I believe they may be the most difficult and dangerous elephants anywhere. Even when Pretorius was here, he often found himself being hunted and forced to run for his life. It is still like that. We will not be allowing cars in here for a long time."

I wondered about the traumatic effect of the Pretorius hunt, and asked him if there were any signs of unusual behavior which could be linked to witnessing family members being killed.

He looked hard at me and answered carefully: "It's funny you should ask that. Most of the adult elephants that survived the 1920 hunt are probably dead by now, and none of the young ones have reason to be so defensive, but they have clearly inherited, or been taught, how and when to be cautious. Even calves of the second post-Pretorius generation share this kind of vigilance. I am not sure what to make of it, but I saw something very odd last month."

I could see he was wondering if he could trust me with a confidence. I said he could and he continued: "We hadn't quite finished the fence. There were several deliberate gaps that needed still to be bridged as soon as a few stray elephants had returned. I was on my own, on foot, keeping a watch on a cow and her male calf in long grass outside the fence. They were upwind of me and feeding quietly until the cow lifted her trunk and tested the air, ears wide.

"She had picked up the sound of one of our work gangs coming along the boundary line, and she began immediately to usher her calf toward the nearest gap in the fence.

"Then the approaching truck backfired, a sound just like a rifle shot, and they panicked. They ran for the gap, the cow leading the way, but the calf misjudged and ended up right on his mother's heels, but separated from her by the fence.

"She stopped, put her trunk through the cables to calm the calf and seemed to be thinking about her next move. There wasn't time to retrace their steps to the opening before the truck arrived. It was only just out of our sight, and she had to do something quickly. I will never be able to prove what happened next, or get my fellow rangers to believe me, but this is what I think took place. . . .

"She talked to that kid. She told him exactly what to do, and without any further fuss, he did. He turned out away from her and the fence and went into the deep shade of a tree twenty yards away, where he stood motionless, becoming virtually invisible. I knew exactly where he was, but could hardly find him again when I looked away. I saw her rush down to the gap and out onto the road, and as the truck appeared, she raised a huge cloud of dust, stamping and blowing, making short charges at the vehicle, frightening the crew sufficiently to get them to back off and go away. Which they did, reversing rapidly as she matched them, yard for yard. And when the noise and confusion was at its height, the calf in camouflage made his move. He sidled over to the fence, slipped quietly through the gap, and went over to wait in the cover of the succulent forest.

I was certain then that the cow's entire performance had been a brilliant diversion, beautifully executed, for as soon as she was sure he had made good his escape, she ignored the truck and its occupants and turned her back, sashaying in satisfaction back to join her calf in the safety of the park. I felt like applauding!"

ELEPHANTS are like that. It is hard not to describe their behavior in human terms, to see ourselves and our foibles in them.

As you get to know them, elephant faces become strangely familiar and you begin to notice very subtle changes of expression. They seem sometimes to smile and other times to wrinkle their foreheads and shake their heads in annoyance. And they definitely have a fine, loose-boned saunter when they have reason to be particularly pleased with themselves. They regularly play games, chasing invisible foes, indulging in elaborate water sports, and showing all the signs that in humans we never hesitate to identify as evidence of self-awareness. Joyce Poole has no doubts about it. She says: "I often get the very strong feeling that they see themselves as large, rather comical animals . . . and seem to do things for their own or others' amusement. Elephants are clowns and give every indication of being aware of it."

Perhaps we shouldn't be so afraid of anthropomorphism. Objectivity is all very well and scientific, but is it good science not to give elephants, and a number of other animals, the benefit of the doubt when it comes to the possession of consciousness? We do so for our own babies because the failure to do so, for either species, runs the risk of depriving ourselves altogther of any chance of better understanding.

At the age of fifteen, such philosophical issues were new to me, but the ranger's story touched a chord. It made sense of what little I knew from watching elephants on the edge of the Kruger National Park, and made me wonder about the Addo herd and their particular experience. Elephants everywhere exercise escape responses and defensive behavior in ways that protect them from traditional enemies such as lions or tigers. Such behavior patterns are innate, built-in, passed down from generation to generation through the genes. Their avoidance of humans, especially in the Addo, must be something relatively new. Something not so much genetic as based on individual or herd experience. The ranger's story supported the probability of learned behavior being communicated directly, by example and encouragement, from parent elephants to their calves. But was it not also possible, in a species with such a long time between generations, that evolution could find advantage in selecting for some other way of transmitting novel and useful information?

Before getting any deeper into biological heresy, I needed more information. I needed to see the Addo elephants for myself. . . .

WHEN the Addo Elephant Park was enclosed, there were about twenty elephants in the herd. Nobody was sure of the exact number. To justify the existence of the park, it was important that people be able to see them, even if only for a moment. So earth mounds were raised at several points on the perimeter and oranges, pineapples, and pumpkins put out at the main viewing ramp each evening. These always vanished overnight, and before long a few of the bolder elephants were turning up at dusk to take early advantage of this regular meal.

I kept the same appointment myself, every day for a week, and was finally rewarded with a good view of a herd bull and two adult females. They materialized out of the succulent wilderness without warning, like ghosts in the gloaming, drifting into view without a sound. One moment the glade was empty and in the next, there they were, in single file, heads swaying, trunks stretching forward to test the ground. Several times they stopped, listening, the leading female holding them there in silence until she was certain it was safe to go on.

The light was going fast, but I could see them clearly, and my first impression was that they were not quite like elephants further north. They seemed smaller, more dense, as though their stature had been reframed to suit the environment, so that no broad head or back rose above the height of the bacon tree jungle. They were still obviously African elephants, *Loxodonta africana*, the same species as everywhere else on the savanna, but I struggled to define the difference.

They were bright red for a start, but that was to be expected in this area of rusty soils. They also had an angular aspect, not clumsy, but slightly off-key, the result perhaps of tension born of generations of persecution. They looked ill-at-ease, which is a very subjective and unsatisfactory assessment, but my attention shifted almost immediately to another oddity. I knew there was something missing, but couldn't put my finger on it until I realized that neither of the females had tusks and that those of the bull were unusually thin and short for an adult.

John Pringle later confirmed this impression. "That worried Pretorius too. Part of his contractual agreement with the province was that he would be allowed to keep the ivory, and he soon discovered that there was very little. Scarcely a dozen decent tusks from the entire enterprise. Those of the bulls were greatly reduced, and the cows had no tusks at all. I had the chance to look at one dead female and found that there was no sign of tusk growth, even under the skin. Where you would usually find at least a stump or root point on the jaw, there was absolutely nothing but solid bone. I suspect that there is no use for tusks in the Addo. All the vegetation, thick as it is, is succulent and soft. There are no trees with hard wood, no branches to break, and nothing to dig for. So, in time, tusks have become redundant. The male elephants seem to have kept theirs only as a matter of pride, for sexual attraction, like showy mustaches!"

THAT made sense. Nature is seldom if ever profligate or wasteful. If the resources required to achieve any result are greater than the benefits, that line of development breaks down. The behavior stops, the structures involved dwindle and disappear. They no longer make sense and are discontinued.

A survey of elephants in East Africa in the 1930s found that just 1 percent of all adults were tuskless. This was regarded as a rare mutation, but twenty years later a similar study found that the figure was nearer 30 percent. All over Africa, particularly where elephants have been hunted for centuries, there is a timely trend toward having smaller tusks. It is rare now to find "big tuskers" anywhere in West Africa, for instance. Part of the explanation lies in genetics. There has been a selective pressure applied by hunters and poachers so that all elephants with genes that produce big tusks have been removed from the population.

If elephants are given full protection, big tusks might return in time, because in some areas they still represent an adaptation that has survival value. That is why bulls with big tusks developed in the first place. They are very sexy and successful. But in the Addo, there are other priorities. Having small tusks or no tusks at all is a useful evolutionary strategy, coming to the rescue of beleaguered herds. And a bad attitude is equally effective. If a population gets a reputation for being ill-tempered and dangerous as well as tuskless, hunters tend to find that killing them is just not worth the risk.

It is not easy to see how outrage, if it can be called that, can be perpetuated down through the generations without being renewed by more recent provocation. The Addo Park was becoming a far more secure environment for elephants, and they did appear to be somewhat calmer as a result. With less to be nervous about, new calves were being born, but something I saw on my last day there got me thinking.

The physical scars left by Major Pretorius were still visible, even after thirty years. Everywhere in the Addo, old limb bones project from the bushes or lie bleaching in the sun where elephants must come across them from time to time. I actually saw a young bull stop near the fence to examine a skull with what looked like nervous concern. He put the tip of his trunk into the head cavities again and again, slowly and carefully as if in a trance. Trying to recall a familar smell? Or something familial, perhaps? Or could it be more than curiosity, maybe a kind of homage? A kind of remembrance for a species with long memories. A ceremony, lest we forget. . . .

Who knows what ancient depths exist or what new ploys are coming into play as elephants everywhere are having to struggle to survive? And was I wrong in feeling that the Addo, as part of the stimulating Cape coastal system, was actually a very good place to look for new and inventive strategies? New elephantine ideas.

The more I thought about it, the more convinced I became that the Cape was some sort of crucible, an alchemical laboratory, not just for elephants, but also for people. A place where almost anything could happen. The presence of more then eight thousand unique plant species is just the substrate for staggering biodiversity. It supports what Jan Smuts once called "the ladder of the soul," an awesome interconnection of living things, each a small part of something far greater and infinitely surprising.

I sensed something of this in the seed of little more than a dozen elephants rescued and implanted in the new park. A new beginning. Something strange and hopeful, and, with this in mind, I decided to have a look at the Cape's other embattled herd.

I kept a promise to myself and returned to Knysna. . . .

ELEPHANTS were once widespread in South Africa, perhaps 100,000 of them, foraging along the river courses, following the rains and the forest margins, gathering in good times wherever food was most plentiful. We know, from the continued existence of desert elephants on the Skeleton Coast, that they can and will travel long dry distances to find what they need. But as the climate became less kind and they ran into human competition, elephants began to concentrate in the subtropical north and behind the geographical barrier of the folded mountains of the southern Cape, particularly in the temperate coastal forest that once stretched all the way from the Addo to Knysna.

By the beginning of the colonial period in the sixteenth century, this ecology had already begun to fragment. The Khoi had arrived with their herds of cattle and sheep. Fires, both natural and deliberately set, took their toll, and the elephants became less migratory, settling on core territories of denser vegetation in the area between the Kaaimans River and the Storms River.

Human settlements since the Ice Age have captured the Cape Coast in interriverine parcels. With the Outeniqua and Tsitsikamma Mountains to the north and the Indian Ocean to the south, the only barriers on the coastal plain were deep and densely forested valleys every thirty miles or so. And all these sectors are still marked on maps as natural entities enclosing settlements, nature reserves, and forest stations with names like Gouna, Keurboom, and Whiskey Creek that recognize their Khoi, Afrikaans, and English origins.

Four hundred years ago, there may have been as many as a thousand elephants here. The first Europeans to arrive in the middle of the eighteenth century were pioneer travelers such as the dour Swedish botanist Carl Thunberg and the effervescent French ornithologist François le Vaillant. The former complained about elephants that rudely interrupted his plant-collecting. The latter was full of Gallic enthusiasm about elephant meat stewed in the pot of its own foot: "I could not conceive that so gross and heavy an animal as the elephant would afford such delicate fare." Neither made any serious attempt to estimate the elephant population, but both made so much of the glories of the forest that they were very soon followed by hordes of woodcutters who plied their trade there for the next 150 years.

Felling, hand sawing in open pits, and hauling of rough planks on sleds pulled by oxen to the sea all began in earnest in 1812 when the Royal Navy ordered supplies. And peaked again in 1836 with the Great Trek of Dutch settlers, disenchanted with British rule at the Cape, and their demand for good wood to build wagons. Before long the ax and the gun dominated the scene. The pastoral Outeniqua Khoi, the Honey People, were soon dispossessed, becoming a people without a purpose or a place, and the elephants retreated to the deepest parts of the forest.

By 1847, all the easily available timber had been cut and the crown forests were closed. The little logging camp at Knysna—the name derives from a Khoi word that means "a hard place to get to" —became isolated again, and the elephants enjoyed a brief reprieve. But in 1871, Thomas Bain, an engineer so successful at road-building he became known as the Colossus of Roads, cut into the side of a hill in the Knysna forest and uncovered a wide vein of quartz which proved a few years later to contain gold. By 1885, more than two thousand claims were being worked on behalf of forty syndicates—and the peace of the forest was shattered forever.

I HAD been away from Knysna for just three years, but fifteen-year-old eyes are very different from those of a twelve-year-old, and I had some catching up to do.

In the small stone library in the center of the village I found some fascinating history. In 1867, His Royal Highness the Duke of Edinburgh, second son of Queen Victoria, came to Knysna on a private visit. He made a good start, arriving off the coast on a Royal Navy vessel and being rowed into the lagoon through a cut in the ancient marine terracing known as the Knysna Heads. He was apparently enchanted by the scenery: "In some places you see hill rising behind hill, like billows on the sea, each fainter in the distance, and each clothed with dark, glossy evergreen woods. In others, you have glens where lofty trees of giant growth, heavy with lichens, support their living roof of leaf-clad branches high overhead, whilst a tangled wilderness of underwood, itself composed of trees and tree-like creepers, fills the space between."

That's as good a travel note as Knysna ever got, but the next day the twenty-three-year-old Prince Alfred spoilt the effect by killing two elephants and fatally wounding at least two other members of a herd of eleven "brutes."

In 1876, Thomas Bain, who built good roads at the astonishing rate of thirty miles a year and was obviously a man to trust, estimated that there appeared to be between four and five hundred elephants in the forest areas where he worked. Using this information, Captain Christopher Harison, the Conservator of Forests, suggested to the Cape government that it was time to protect the surviving elephants. The government turned down this suggestion as frivolous, and the carnage continued as licenses were issued freely to people like Rear Admiral Robert Morris, or anyone else who had a gun and would travel. By 1902, it had to be officially admitted that the herd was reduced to less than fifty, but it was not until 1908 that the elephants were proclaimed Royal Game.

Fortunately no further Royals passed by, but the Knysna Forest Department had no authority to stop hunters, who were still being issued free licenses in Cape Town, and the decline continued to just thirteen known animals when war broke out in 1914. The herd bounced back to seventeen during that distant hostility, but with the armistice came the ultimate lunacy. The Provincial Adminstrator, for reasons that remain entirely unclear, authorized the shooting of one of the last Knysna elephants "for science." And the hunter so honored was, of all people, Major P. J. Pretorius, fresh from his triumph in the Addo!

SUCH foolishness made me feel angry, and silly for feeling angry more than thirty years after the event. But my dismay deepened even further when I discovered the whole story. . . .

Pretorius, it seemed, had promised the South African Museum "tuskers of the most abnormal proportions" from the Addo hunt. Such elephants, of course, didn't exist in the Addo, and all the museum received was a motley collection of material from small elephants, without tusks, or with tiny tusks that didn't fit the heads received and already paid for. The British Museum was no better served, and both entered into long and acrimonious correspondence with Pretorius. The net outcome was that the two museums combined received the poorly prepared and poorly documented remains of just six elephants from the hundred or more Pretorius killed in the Addo. And it is clear now that his reason for asking to be allowed to kill a Knysna bull in addition was not science, but injured pride, and perhaps the hope that he could find something big enough to make good on his earlier promises and avoid legal action by the museums.

Pretorius let it be known that he would go to Knysna to see if the race of elephants there was the same as that in the Addo. "It would be of great interest for science," he suggested, "and I can prove this fact if I can see the Knysna elephants. I propose going there on my own expense and may find it necessary to shoot one." He would, wouldn't he.

The Cape Adminstrator leaned over backward: "Help yourself. I will instruct the Conservator of Forests at Knysna to facilitate your visit in every way. By all means kill an elephant, if necessary. And if at all possible, make it one old bull because the number remaining is very small."

Pretorius came to kill, not just to see, and the result was a disaster from which the Knysna herd may never recover.

It began on July 9, 1920, at the hotel in George, near Knysna. Word had got out that an elephant hunt was to take place, and when Pretorius arrived with his wife, a photographer named Joe Albrechts, three servants, and a pack of dogs, there was an excited crowd. Pretorius loved the attention, and when he overheard some of the women whispering to each other that they would love to go with him, he invited "anyone who wishes" to come along.

So, after breakfast the following day, a whole circus, including a mountaineering excursion from Cape Town consisting of five girls, set out in convoy on a seven-mile drive over muddy roads. At the Millwood Forest Station they were joined by the Chief Forester and a local hunter named John Keet, together with a tribe of beaters, who all trooped into the forest following an elephant path for another five miles to where the herd had last been seen. There they pitched camp, and the hunt itself came to a climax on the third day. There are several accounts of what happened, all differing in vital details, and none quite corroborating Pretorius's own story. But the local press reports I read, all vividly written in a flowing narrative style that puts today's newspapers to shame, present a compelling picture of the whole inglorious episode.

IN his own self-serving autobiography, *Jungle Man,* Pretorius makes light of the opening moves: "The Chief Forester took the dogs and set off. When we reached the spot where the elephants had been seen they loosed the hounds. At once the dogs picked up the spoor, and scarcely a minute later the shrill sound of barking reached us. Next I heard the elephants, and then came the sound of breaking trees as the great beasts approached the spot where we were standing in wait with the cameras."

A good beginning, but what is missing here right at the start is an event which Pretorius, for obvious reasons, never mentioned. The gap, however, is filled by two of the excursionists whom he himself had invited to witness his triumph. One was the delightfully named Miss Cuckoo Lister, presumably one of the Cape Town mountaineers, who spoke to the *Millwood Museum Newsletter*:

"We climbed the little hill above the camp and there on the opposite slope across the river was the whole herd feeding in a glade between two little forests in the kloof. The Major quietly arranged matters, told us we could stay to watch the proceedings, out of range of the bullets, and he and Mrs. Pretorius, who acted as his gunbearer, and Mr. Albrecht the photographer, took up their position in the opposite glade. We were within shouting distance and had a perfect view.

"John Keet and the Forester then took a tribe of beaters to the next glade and there suddenly came face to face with the whole herd. One cow elephant charged them so John fired at her and wounded her and then we saw the whole herd career down the slope and all the beaters and us yelling for all we were worth."

No mention of the dogs, but these reappear in another version given by Francis Newdigate of Knysna to the *Cape Argus*:

"Trees began to sway and shake, dogs started yelping madly, people shouted and then, as the noise seemed to be at its height, the heavens were rent with the most terrible racket imaginable—the fierce trumpeting of elephants in distress, for the dogs were attacking a cow and her calf, and the mother was furious."

We learn in this way that the charge by the cow was no accident. She had a calf and was already being beset by the dogs. John Keet could have fired in the air, but it is unfair to second-guess a man faced with an irate mother elephant. The initial aggression was the decision by Pretorius to grandstand by sending in the beaters and his hounds.

Pretorius, meanwhile, was waiting on the prepared killing ground, where, he said: "Fortune favoured us. The leader of the herd was a huge bull, who suddenly appeared thirty yards away. He put up his ears, raised his trunk and charged. I hit him, at a range of twenty paces, but my bullet did not turn him; he still came forward. Albrecht stuck to his camera. I had to shoot again, and this time put a bullet in his ear which dropped him."

All very heroic and matter-of-fact, but the witnesses saw something rather different. Cuckoo Lister: "The great bull emerged first, just below Pretorius, and he fired at it *in the back so as to get a good cinema picture* [my emphasis]. It dashed on across to the next little forest in spite of another bullet in the head."

So much for dropping the first bull in his tracks. Francis Newdigate fills in the picture: "We all looked tensely at Pretorius, and as we gazed, out into the open walked the most magnificent elephant we had ever seen, not fifty yards from him. This, then, must have been the bull that Pretorius had hoped to get. The sight of the monstrous animal and the wiry little man facing each other was a contrast never to be forgotten. Neither feared the other and as the bull walked past, ears extended and trunk held high, there was contempt for man in every stride he took. Then the camera got busy and Pretorius stepped out. BANG! and a cloud of dust appeared on the elephant's back where the bullet struck it. With a sort of stumble the old bull continued his walk. Yet another BANG!, but the large bore, high velocity express elephant rifle seemed to have little effect."

Everyone agrees about the first two shots being fired, but there is nothing to support the impression Pretorius gives of a direct charge by the bull. On the contrary, it seems instead to have been walking by with its ears wide and trunk high—the usual signs of an alert, but not aggressive elephant. Pretorius never fired in self-defense, and both witnesses describe a scene scripted for the camera, an encounter designed to provide commercial footage, not scientific information. Pretorius needed an adult bull elephant and some promotional material and got both in two shots, but not just with two bullets!

PRETORIUS, however, got another chance to shine. "While I was still concentrating on the first bull, the party yelled. I turned and saw another bull charging straight toward the camera. I let drive and gave him a bullet in the head which dropped him, but it was not a fatal shot, and he quickly rose. The next time I fired at his brain, and he fell dead."

But did he? Francis Newdigate says it took six shots to kill the second elephant, and that this occurred before Pretorius had the time to follow up and finally dispatch the first. Cuckoo Lister agrees: "Meantime, to our horror, another huge chap came out about thirty yards above Major Pretorius and Mrs. Pretorius, so we yelled and they looked round to find this elephant charging them. The cine was quickly concentrated on that and Pretorius fired. The elephant turned and also made for the forest, the Major, his wife and the cine man hard on his heels. They put an end to him there and then hurried down and finished off the other one."

That took eight shots and ended, according to Newdigate, only when "Pretorius jumped on his body and stood there in triumph. The bull raised his head to look at his gloating enemy and rolled on his side without a sound or a struggle, as becoming the passing of so noble a creature."

Bringing the score to one cow wounded with one shot from John Keet, and two bulls killed with fourteen shots by Major Pretorius. Measurements were made and photographs taken, but the day was not over yet. . . .

The remainder of the terror-stricken herd fled, but in the process one calf slipped onto a shelf halfway down a cliff face, and while trying to save it, a forester and the beaters were attacked by the mother, who was also fired on. She was found dead of her wounds the following day, twelve miles away. The calf too died, as did another, presumed to be the child of the first cow wounded, probably fatally. A total of two bulls, two calves, and at least one cow—a full house out of a herd of seven elephants, from a population of no more than seventeen animals. Making Pretorius the butcher who tore the heart out of both the last Cape herds—all for nothing.

He claimed that the larger of the two bulls he killed at Knysna was twelve feet six inches tall at the shoulder and boasted that "there was not at that time another such elephant in any museum in the world." There still isn't. By the time his prize specimen reached the British Museum, the much-vaunted giant was found to be no more than nine feet three inches tall . . . and altogether ordinary.

No one shot Philip Jacobus Pretorius. He died aged sixty-two in 1945, a decade before I even knew he existed. He was a child of his time, as I am of mine. Things looked different then, but it is hard to come to terms with a man who had so little affinity for life that he chose to deal in death. And hard to forgive a man who can have himself photographed sitting on a heap of dead elephants looking pleased with himself and referring to the corpses as "Dumbos."

After this catalog of horrors in the Knysna library, I needed an antidote, something to clear my mind of dead elephants and renew the magic of ones still alive and surprising. I went out into a nearby part of the forest called the Garden of Eden and wandered along an elephant walk worn smooth by centuries of large soft feet. I didn't see or hear any elephants. I hardly expected to in this small sample of a six-hundred-square-mile range. But as soon as I entered the cathedral grove of a group of giant yellowwoods, I was beset by the possibility of elephants, by a certain expectant sense I remembered from Strandloper days of the presence of elephants somewhere nearby.

It has nothing to do with the usual feelers we put out to explore the world around us. These are frustrated anyway in forest such as this by an inability to see very far or hear much in foliage so dense it blankets the senses. It is more like expectancy, a heightened awareness produced at first by the knowledge that there *are* elephants around, but sharpened also by something else, by a vibrance that just doesn't exist anywhere in those empty places now without elephants in them.

There is no mistaking the feeling, and I surrendered to it, enjoying the pleasures of association. Running my fingers over the broad waxy leaves of candlewood elephants like to browse; picking up the purple berries of the Cape beech, whose wood is treasured by local makers of violins; wading through thickets of soft tree fern, any of which could conceal an entire elephant herd; listening to the clear, high pitched call of a chorus of ghost frogs, and hoping for the hoarse, descending call of the Knysna *lourie* that ends in a hiss, warning elephants of a potential intrusion.

I realized that, pleasant as it was to walk on my own, I needed local guidance to help me actually see one of the few remaining elephants. By the mid-1950s, the herd had shrunk to fewer than ten elephants. Dead calves had been found in 1931, 1937, and 1942—intervals that coincide with the calving sequence so closely that the deaths could be disasters befalling just one breeding female. A lone bull was being sighted regularly in the crags of Deepwalls, but several short surveys had not been able to find the tracks of more than three other individuals. The foresters themselves, however, felt that there were other, more canny elephants still lurking in the unlogged ravines, bringing the total to perhaps eight or nine.

I asked for assistance from the District Forest Offices and was gently steered away from the subject. They had been badgered too often by irate farmers or concerned conservationists to find the mention of elephants at all comfortable, but their reluctance was tempered by one prevailing piece of advice. If I wanted to see elephants, unofficially, I would have to find a tracker. One of those whose family had lived in and on the forest for generations, making a tenuous and indentured living delivering cut timber to the Knysna sawmills. What I needed was a woodcutter—one of the reclusive breed known locally as *houtkappers*.

WHEN interest in the forests was first aroused by travelers such as the effusive François le Vaillant, all shipping to the east went around the Cape and timber was in demand for spars and hull repairs. Knysna promised to meet that need, and in 1776, Forestry Department Posts were established at George, Knysna, and Plettenberg Bay. Each of these housed a Resident, whose task it was "to superintend the Government Woods and Forests."

Easier said than done. Thousands of men with oxen and axes poured into the forests, and the Forestry Department's only control over them was at the market end on the posts. There the Residents bought the timber on the "good for" system, with flour, sugar, coffee, and tobacco, holding the cutters in permanent debt, keeping them guessing about the value of their wares, belittling the quality of the timber brought in, demanding the impossible. If the *houtkappers* brought in stinkwood, the resident wanted yellowwood for railway sleepers. If they came with candlewood wheel spokes, he needed ironwood for *disselbooms* or wagon shafts.

And so it went. The woodcutters squatted on land they didn't own deep in the forest. They lived on sweet potatoes, brown bread, and black coffee in hillbilly hovels with a few pigs and chickens, seldom seeing outsiders, learning nothing but their trade, fearing God and the elephants they called "bigfeet."

Their independence was all they had. The work was backbreaking, cutting, dragging, sawing, but they worked when they

liked and as little as they pleased, and they had each other. They
intermarried exclusively amongst a handful of families—Van
Rooyen, Stroebel, Barnard, and Terblans—speaking a kind of trade
Afrikaans. They were generally fatalistic, but grew increasingly
uneasy about encroaching civilization.

In 1873, the first Conservator of Forests ended this happy-
go-lucky way of life. The *houtkappers'* cavalier attitude to logging was
causing irreparable damage to all the most accessible parts of the forest. So Captain Harison set the first organized approach to logging in
train, and by 1914, access to the forest was limited to a far smaller
number of woodcutters, all registered and licensed and given specific
quotas that provided just enough for each family to live on. The rest,
with reluctance, entered the general labor pool, where they were
joined in 1939 by the last of the *houtkappers*, pensioned off as their
rights were annulled. But they never disappeared altogether. . . .

Members of all the leading forest families were still to be found
in various trades in Knysna and were easily identified. They tended
to be tall in a rangy way, elongated perhaps by generations who
experienced daylight only sparingly as it diffused through the forest
canopy. Some still worked, as they always had, in waistcoat, braces,
and a felt hat. Off duty, they seemed always to be surrounded by
their extended families, somewhat solemn and careful in speech and
demeanor, slow to express an opinion and scornful of any suggestion of knowing something not learned firsthand.

My inquiries around the village about someone who knew about
elephants kept turning in the same direction: "Kroos Arend is the
man you want to see," everyone said. "He works in the timberyard
on Thesen's Island." So I crossed the causeway in the lagoon and
went in search of this man whose name translated promisingly as
"Offspring of the Eagle."

Boats were being built on the island, and near where the keels
were being laid I passed a huge old frame saw rocking its way
through baulks of timber. Beyond that, on the water's edge, was the

quietest part of yard, an old shed called the Stinkwood Store. Here, piled high one upon another, were thousands of planks all neatly packed to allow air to pass between them and carry away the sour smell of this precious dark wood, used almost exclusively for the finest furniture. And working amongst these stacks was someone wearing the usual forest uniform and a misshapen hat.

I waited for him to finish what he was doing. He did, in his own good time, moving with the deliberation of a man used to being old and knowing his own limitations.

Eventually he finished, straightened up, and turned to look at me with eyes very like an eagle's, clear brown, bright and piercing. Eyes that had seen it all and still found it interesting, and between them, a sharp aquiline nose.

"Kroos Arend," I confirmed. He lifted his head a fraction in acknowledgment. The demeanor of a man who knows who he is and is comfortable with it. I prepared to explain myself, but he silenced me with a soft gesture and shaped his mouth in the way that some quiet men do when they are about to say something.

Finally, he said, in Afrikaans: "I know what you want. This is a small town and there are few secrets. News here travels like a wind that tries to blow in both directions. Mostly I don't pay any attention, but I listened to what I heard about you. And I can help you, but I need first to know one thing. . . ."

I looked at him expectantly and he continued: "Have you ever seen a white elephant?"

The shock in my eyes was answer enough.

"Good. So, meet me tomorrow. Early, at the Big Tree."

CHAPTER FIVE

Tracking the Elephant

I have seen a herd of elephants travelling through
the native forest, pacing along as if they had an
appointment at the end of the world.
—Isak Dinesen in *Out of Africa*, 1937

THE giants of the Knysna forest are not the elephants, but soaring
yellowwood trees with elegant crowns of branches bearing narrowly
elliptic dark green leaves and festoons of gray-green lichen. And the
largest specimen left, 140 feet tall and measuring almost thirty feet
around its trunk, is known simply as the Big Tree. It is said to be
perhaps eight hundred years old and stands on its own, by the side
of the road in Deepwalls, given a little breathing room by the clear-
ance of the area around its giant buttressed feet. Everything else, by
comparison, is undergrowth.

I arrived at dawn, with a forest mist clinging to the canopy,
and found that Kroos Arend was already waiting for me, leaning
with his back against the tree trunk in exactly the same way
!Kamma had done three years before. He was humming, or perhaps praying, in a soft monotone, so I approached quietly and

again stood waiting until he greeted me, still with his eyes closed.

"*Goie more.* I'm telling this old tree, this *kalander,* about you. It pays to be polite. He will spread the word without words, which is important. In this forest, you must never say the name of that you seek. To do so would set them looking for us, and you never know how a bigfoot might respond."

He looked different today. The clothes were the same, but the eyes were brighter still, animating his old face in ways that made him seem far younger than I knew he had to be. The last woodcutters were laid off before the Second World War, at about the time I was born, and Kroos, by all accounts, was then already a grandfather, the patriarch of his people.

"*Kom,*" he said, turning away from the Big Tree with a long last glance up into its crown. "We still have a way to go to Askoekheuwel."

I liked the sound of that. Ashcake Hill! The forest was full of *houtkapper* memories kept alive by names like Velbroeksdraai and Broedertwis—"Skintrouser Bend" and "Falling-out of Brothers." Most of these were virtual places, marked by nothing but a name. Nothing to see when you got there except forest reclaiming its own, but each such mark in the mind was part of a network of tradition that held the forest together as surely as the hills on which it grew.

As we walked, Kroos drew my attention to things I might otherwise have missed. A slow-growing white pear tree with its slender V-shaped crown. The "cherooo-weet" call of an orange-throated Cape robin. A closely knit bag of papery white silk and dead leaves which marked the nest of a large, fast-moving rain spider.

I was entranced. We moved easily through the undergrowth on what looked like an old sled trail, heading west, though it was hard to be certain of direction when we got only occasional glimpses of the sun. But after about half an hour, our path intersected with a different kind of track, narrower, cleaner, kept clear by some other agency. An elephant walk.

Kroos turned right, northward, on this ancient right-of-way, and almost immediately we found them. Large, even indentations in the pathway, their outlines crisp in the moist early-morning air. Fresh elephant tracks!

Kroos stopped and crouched, looking down the line of stride. He traced the oval outline of a forefoot, pointed at the deeper, more cylindrical print of a hind foot with its characteristic trailing scuff, and picked up a little of the loosened earth, rolling it gently between thumb and forefinger, finally lifting it up to his eaglelike nose.

"An adult cow," he said. "Last night. Coming from the Steenbras River and headed for Kom se Pad. I know this lady. She is somewhat shy, usually on her own, and often very angry. Keep your eyes open for trees that can easily be climbed!"

TRACKING cannot just be taught. It is something that is done, an ongoing process of problem-solving which requires not only wide field experience, but a great deal of imagination.

Good trackers don't only read tracks, they also read very carefully between the visible lines, looking not *at* a trail, but *into* it. Trackers know the tricks of the trade—working if they can in low-angle light at dawn or dusk, seldom looking straight down at their feet, but up ahead, anticipating, looking beyond what can immediately be seen. And the best of them seem to have short attention spans, showing only intermittent interest in the footprints on the sand, refocusing constantly on other lines of evidence, juggling with information in a way that gives them an ever-changing overview of the whole story.

Louis Liebenberg, a South African biologist and archaeologist, believes that tracking may well be the oldest science, something that involves the same intellectual processes as modern science. He sug-

gests that, like tracking, all science still tries to explain the visible
world by calling on an invisible model. The observable properties of
any problem are, just like spoor, the signs of invisible processes.
Understanding them requires not just careful observation, but the
use of pure imagination. So even subatomic physicists "hunt" par-
ticles, studying "tracks" in bubble chambers, talking optimistically
about "closing in on their quarry."

Good science, like good tracking, also requires intuition—which
Liebenberg defines as "reaching a conclusion on the basis of less
explicit information than is ordinarily required." Such leaps of
imagination look more like magic than science, but they are very
real and useful steps in most processes of discovery. Nothing truly
novel comes from established knowledge alone. That can become
dogmatic and authoritarian, creating infallible facts and frameworks
which are not subject to discussion. Most textbooks don't prepare
one for fresh approaches. They leave out the leaps of faith that lead
to true breakthroughs.

A tracker in action has to think and feel like the animal he tracks.
He has to have empathy and a trust in the sort of intuitive feelings that
some describe as a "burning sensation" in the center of their foreheads, or as a "tapping at the ribs." Such physiological responses may
be due to peripheral perceptions, to unconscious awareness of things
too subtle to come to consciousness. Such signs tend to accumulate
somewhere in the old brain, lurking there until there are enough of
them to overflow into our busy new forebrains. There they demand
attention. Coming apparently out of nowhere, they seem mysterious
and are often ignored, but not by anyone whose life may depend on
reading a trail accurately and using it to make a useful prediction.

Tracking began a long time ago, probably before we became
human. The process was initially a simple one, just following a trail
by sight or smell, but it soon became more systematic, involving the
gathering of other information. Such an activity requires logic and
reason and presumes a fairly high level of cerebral development,

but the final stage of tracking is quite different in nature. It demands anticipation, speculation, and prediction, and that seems to limit it to humans, but there is good reason to believe that such talent is not ours alone. We may share it with elephants.

KROOS AREND was an extraordinary tracker.

To begin with, the trail left by the solitary female was easy to follow. Her prints were clearly visible on the old elephant walk. But before we reached the road at Kom se Pad, she turned off into the undergrowth and headed west. Kroos started off slowly, casting around for broken ferns and signs of browsing, but soon picked up pace, marching along at something approaching elephant speed.

"*Sowaar,*" he said confidently. "Truly, she is going now to the Gouna River. There are good pools there in the *kloof*, before McFarlane's Eiland." He spat. "I know she likes to bathe there!"

An *eiland*—or island—in the forest is not surrounded by water, it is a piece of higher ground surrounded by a sea of trees. And McFarlane, it appeared, was an early Resident or wood buyer who was not very popular with the *houtkappers*.

Kroos pointed out a kite spider, a very colorful and crustacean-looking female as big as my thumbnail, who was busy repairing her orb web. "The bigfoot passed here in the dark, probably just before dawn. The web was broken and it is too high off the ground to have been damaged by a bushbuck. And the little *spinnekop* would not have started to repair her trap until daylight."

I looked impressed, but he waved away my admiration. "*Toemaar*—never mind that," he said. "You have to see. Just look and you will not learn. Your head will be only half full. And you have to look for signs all around, not just on the ground ahead of you."

I began to look around with new enthusiasm, exploring the forest understory and even the canopy above me for vital signs—and promptly fell over a huge pile of elephant droppings that lay steaming in the path. Kroos broke a lifetime of woodcutter reserve and cackled like a guinea fowl. I was astonished and looked hard at him, but by then he had stopped himself, a large scarred hand covering his mouth for the impropriety of it, but the brightness in his eyes was unmistakable and we both broke out laughing out loud.

"Never walk in the tracks of an animal," he admonished. "Walk to one side in case you lose the trail and have to backtrack."

I wiped my boots with a fern leaf and looked at the dung with interest. Each bolus was huge, cannonball size, and held together by fibers of the foods the elephant had been eating. I broke one of the balls open and discovered that the contents were only partly digested. With a hand lens, you could still identify every plant.

"Young bigfeet have at least two grinding teeth on each side of both jaws. Enough to chew their food well. As they get older, they have only one tooth there at a time, and as these wear down, they do a poor job and the animals digest less and lose weight. Kroos looked at the ball I had broken and continued: "She is fine. In her prime, but *prikkelbaar*—irritable—I think because she lost her last calf."

As he spoke, I continued to examine the impressive pile of droppings and was suddenly aware that I was not the only admirer. Right at my feet, a large black beetle was nosing at the heap, making excited little movements at its edge, testing its consistency.

Kroos was amused. "*Misstamper*. It doesn't take them long to get here. They follow the bigfeet and tidy up after them."

ELEPHANTS are prodigious eaters, taking in more then three hundred pounds of vegetation every day. The processing of this takes between one and two days as it passes through 120 feet of intestine, losing about half its weight as it goes. Digestion is always incomplete, mainly because of a surprising lack of symbiotic bacteria in the gut. Most of this internal fauna and flora flourishes in an appendix five feet long, and the function of the stomach and long intestine seems to be largely one of absorbing water.

So 60 percent of what an elephant eats, nearly two hundred pounds of partly digested vegetable matter, ends up on the forest floor, including the undamaged seeds of bushes, trees, and grasses carried miles away from their source and deposited, not just in new territory, but in an excellent nutrient medium. Some species, such as the hard redwood tree *makoré*, are now found only along historic elephant routes in eastern and central Africa and have no known origin.

The same may be true of ourselves. We seem to be children of the savanna, weaned from the trees ten million years ago and turned loose to spend our seed in the open spaces. But both we and the savanna are latecomers to Africa. Neither would exist at all were it not for the preexistence of a natural force which started crafting Africa's landscape and shaping its ecology some fifty million years before.

Elephants have a considerable impact on the land. They leave shrubs uprooted and trees debarked, killing many species faster than they can regenerate. This is often viewed as "the elephant problem," but only by those who still believe that elephants and trees existed in stable equilibrium until we came along and interfered with their ranges and migration routes. Not so. Recent surveys of just one species—the upside-down, bulbous, waxy-skinned baobab—have revealed a remarkable pattern. Most living baobabs range from 125 to 200 years old. There are very few younger or older trees, and none between the age of twenty-five and fifty. And the architect of this strange design seems to be the elephant.

What it suggests is that elephant populations have always fluctuated, probably because of their close relationship with baobabs and other trees. The system cycles back and forth, with elephants increasing in density as they thin out the forest, and declining again as the trees became too sparse, letting forest regenerate once again. And if the baobab is to be believed, elephants everywhere in Africa were already scarce in the eighteenth century, and most of our more recent experience of them has been confined to a period of recovery.

Elephants, like ourselves, have been involved in massive landscaping projects for a long time, keeping Africa's tropics from going entirely to their moist climax, opening up the forest enough to let us see the trees, and at the same time opening up new habitats and opportunities. Not just for us, but for a whole new ecology that includes key species like the dung beetles.

There are 780 known kinds of dung beetle in South Africa alone, just one branch of the vast army of users and movers of manure. Most of these are scarabs, cousins of the famous Egyptian sacred beetle, symbols of the cyclical process of nature and the endurance of the human soul. And Knysna, of course, has its own distinctive species.

KROOS, who turned out to be a great fan of the interconnectedness of things, showed me that the beetle working busily on our dunghill had peculiar front feet. They ended at the ankle to form broad scoops, perfectly designed to cut and hold and shape a ball of dung larger than the beetle itself. When this is complete, it is rolled laboriously away by the male, who soon attracts a single female.

"It's Friday, and she can hear the money jingling in his pocket," as Kroos put it.

They travel a long way from the drop, rolling along until the male finds the right place to bury his hoard. She follows him into the nuptial chamber, where they mate and spend several days dining on a wedding feast of fresh dung. The honeymoon over, the female goes to work, patting and smoothing a new dung ball until it is perfectly round, depositing just one large egg in a hollow on its side, and then sealing the entrance to the chamber and leaving the larva to hatch and pupate on its own. All very tidy and well designed, serving not only the species but the entire environment.

Kroos enjoyed hearing about what happened when cattle were introduced to ruminant-free Australia and the entire continent was in great danger of being smothered in ordure. The local beetles were not up to the job and had to be supplemented by migrant labor in the form of imported African scarabs, far better equipped for dealing with dung in elephantine proportions.

"Africans always get the shitty jobs," observed Kroos dryly.

In its proper context, elephant dung can be very useful in assessing the numbers of animals in thickly forested areas. Each heap is honest and undeniable proof of the recent existence of at least one elephant in that area. Richard Barnes and his wife, Karen Jensen, working in the Congo Basin, base their estimates on what they call "dung-density data."

These are derived from three measurements: the number of dung piles in each area, the rate of defecation, and the rate of dung decay. The first figure is calculated by walking along carefully drawn transects through the forest on a regular basis, recording every dropping, and taking care not to be confused by the fact that elephants often walk along while defecating, producing droppings in several separate piles. The second figure is the observed average number of dung piles produced per elephant per day, adjusted to allow for the fact that elephants have an interesting habit of always defecating when approaching water. And the third figure is the number of days it takes for a recorded dropping in that area to decay to a predetermined level, at which it is considered not to be a true dropping, but simply humus.

With these figures in hand, all you need is simple arithmetic. The estimated number of elephants is equal to the dung pile density multiplied by the decay rate, divided by the defecation rate. And that's it. In a long series of experiments in thick forest, dung counts have proved to be more accurate than sample counts of the elephants themselves!

In Knysna, it wouldn't help much. The population is so low that such measurements are far less useful. You either have an elephant in your area or you don't. We did, and kept following her trail. . . .

WE were still traveling west in an almost straight line, Askoekheuwel on our left and the Gouna gorge ahead, a gentle breeze blowing toward us. Ideal conditions for tracking. Kroos continued to read the signs, stopping every now and then to listen. All I heard was distant mellow, bubbling phrases from the vast repertoire of a chorister robin, and occasional outbursts of high-pitched cackling from a group of birds Kroos called *kakelaars*, wood hoopoes with curved red bills that travel in parties, flying in straggling procession from tree to tree, picking up and elaborating on the calls of those in the lead until the whole flock collapses in hysterical laughter.

It is a strangely comforting sound. Evidence of conviviality in a forest that is not very welcoming. Especially when you are creeping up on something that weighs ten thousand pounds and is known to be bad-tempered. Visibility is very limited at ground level. Your only long sightlines are directly overhead, into the canopy, which is small consolation. That is the one direction from which an angry elephant is *not* likely to attack you. . . .

I kept looking around for suitable trees to climb. There were woefully few, and just as I was wondering why, from a distance came the noise of a falling tree, loud enough to break the overriding silence suddenly and completely, echoing all around us. Kroos looked at me and nodded. She was where he had expected to find her, in the gorge itself. He glanced up at a break in the canopy, across which we could see soft white clouds moving our way. The wind was still in the right direction, from her to us, so we moved quietly on.

We passed through a patch of tree ferns, several of which were broken, crowns missing or eaten partly away. We kept going, downhill now, stepping over fallen logs, pushing gently through tangles of branches, taking care not to put pressure on anything that would snap. All of which took time, but then there was another sharp crack of breaking branches up ahead, perhaps a hundred yards away where we could see a gap in the roof of green.

Kroos signaled to stop. We did and listened happily to the soothing swishing and crunching sounds of an elephant feeding and, in the background, the tinkling of a tributary of the Gouna. In less than half a day, Kroos had brought me closer to a Knysna elephant than most local people come in a lifetime. She seemed to be totally at ease, unaware of us and moving steadily away downstream, so we followed, hoping to be able to pick up a little height on the edge of the gorge and get a good look down at her from a safe distance. We moved along the south bank, making good progress toward a valley coming in from the left which promised an opening, a break in the forest not far from where she was standing now in the streambed making bathroom noises, sucking and blowing water in and out of her trunk.

It was all very peaceful, almost domestic, and I was beginning to enjoy myself when Kroos stopped dead, rigid, not moving a muscle, his head held high and nostrils flared. I froze. He turned his head slowly left and right, scanning, sniffing, eyes wide and worried, one hand raised to keep me from moving. I didn't think I could move even if I wanted to.

For long, agonizing seconds we held our little tableau, scarcely daring to breathe. I kept my eyes on Kroos, waiting for his cue, wondering what could have disturbed his usual serenity. And was horrified to see a tension in him, even a pallor I would normally attribute to shock, had I not come to believe that this was a man who would take anything in his stride.

Then I saw it in his eyes. He knew what was awry and didn't like it, and in a flash he began to move. Before I knew what was happening, his hand was on my arm, turning me away toward the other side of the gorge, shouting, "Run! *Blitsvinnig*—like lightning! Go!"

We did.

My legs came to independent life and carried me along with them, in a way that seemed likely to clear huge buildings in a single bound. There was no easy, open path, but I have never run as fast or felt so surefooted. Kroos and I, neck and neck, tumbled down the slope toward the creek, slightly upstream of the cow, who watched in amazement as we splashed past her, knee-deep through the water, and began to scramble up the rocks on the far side.

It was a performance impossible to repeat, but what had lent wings to my young legs, and his very much older ones, was what we had both seen just before we fled.

There was a glade at the junction of Gouna and the side valley. It was lighter there, and our path led through it past a wide-spreading Cape ash that leaned partly over on the slope so that part of its crown touched the ground. Kroos had stopped just a few yards from this thicket of large leaves through which nothing could be seen. And over his shoulder, in the instant that he moved, I saw something I will never forget. A wide round forehead, heavily wrinkled between eyes impossibly far apart, burst through the foliage trailing ear flaps big enough to cover a car! It was an enormous bull elephant, head down, trunk tucked between his legs, with a pair of tusks that looked like a snowplow almost scraping the ground. He was moving so fast that he skidded before he could reach full charging speed, and that may be all that saved us.

We could hear the commotion behind us, but never turned to look back. The two of us hit the cliff in a dead heat.

We went up it like monkeys, and by the time I reached the top and gave Kroos a helping hand onto a shelf twenty feet above the stream, our pursuer was already at the base. His trunk reached almost to our heels, but all he could do was blow hot air at us and howl. Trumpeting is too musical a description for that sound. It was terrifying. A wild banshee wail punctuated with grunts of anger and frustration. His whole face was contorted, his eyes huge and wild, showing white all round the iris, which, in its turn, was encircled by an opalescent ring.

There was none of the usual gentle melancholy I had come to expect of elephants. This was a furious animal. His trunk lashed like the tail of an angry cat and he stamped his feet, digging up earth and leaves in a way that seemed to make him even more irate. I have not the least doubt that he would have killed both of us if we had come just a few steps closer. He seemed to have been waiting to do just that. . . .

I was spellbound by the magnitude of such ferocity and jumped when Kroos touched my arm.

"*Gha!* We must go before he finds another way to reach us. We have been very lucky. Do you know who this is?"

I shook my head. As Kroos came to my side, the bull lifted his trunk high and seemed to be picking up a scent that held his interest, keeping him there breathing heavily, but watching us carefully now, ears wide and high as though he understood every word and was waiting to be introduced.

Kroos obliged. "This is Aftand," he said. "He killed my brother."

WE took the easy way back, walking along a logging trail to the Big Tree, and on the way Kroos explained.

"It was in 1939, just before we were forced to leave the forest. Izak was my youngest brother, a true *houtkapper* who loved a challenge. He was the one who made the first and last ax marks on every tree, who could drop a *kalander* on a matchbox without damaging

the trees on either side. He was always the first to volunteer for anything. . . ."

"That year was a dry one. The bigfeet were restless, and we saw
a lot of one big bull, who seemed to be watching everything we did.
He may have been about thirty years old then, just becoming fully
adult and very possessive of his cows. We were the last independent
woodcutters, working under quotas, but our days were numbered.
The foresters were working with chainsaws and heavy machinery
and no longer needed us. I was fifty and ready to retire, but Izak was
eleven years younger, still wanting to work and always *kwaai*—as
angry as any bigfoot in the forest.

"It was inevitable that they would clash, but no one could have
predicted how it would happen. The foresters were clearing a fire-
break through an area known as the Quar, using a bulldozer, making
a terrible noise. But this was the big bull's territory, and he kept shad-
owing the drivers, making everyone very nervous. Except Izak, of
course, who was afraid of nothing except being afraid. He enjoyed the
way the bull was making things difficult for the foresters. In a sense,
they were on the same side, but he nevertheless made up his mind to
show up the foresters by dealing with the fearsome bigfoot directly,
just as he would deal with a giant tree. One man, alone, on foot.

"And it might have worked. Izak had a weapon, an old shotgun
loaded with the solid slugs we used to kill bushpig when they raided
our gardens. He was a good shot, and at close range he could have
done it with several cartridges, but there was something he didn't
know. The bull had chosen the same night for an act of vengeance
of his own.

"He had suffered the invading bulldozer long enough, and
when the last forester had left, he tracked down and attacked the
offending machine.

"He did great battle with it, puncturing all the tires, turning the
monster on its back, and goring it so thoroughly that it bled to death
as diesel flowed from a wound in its belly. *Wragtig*!—truly, he took the

bull right out of the dozer, but in the process broke the end of his left tusk, the one which in many of the Knysna herd curves upward.

"Izak walked into this battleground with nothing more than his gun and another bull, a bullmastiff called Noetzie. We don't know exactly what happened, but from the tracks it was clear that the big-foot with the sore tooth was too fast and too clever. He attacked Izak from ambush in a thicket of tree ferns, gored him several times with his good tusk, and then trampled him to death.

"We knew nothing of this until Noetzie returned home alone and bleeding at dawn. The dog was patched up and led us to what was left of Izak, but there was nothing we could do except just pick up the pieces and hide the gun. We never told anyone else. There was no love lost between *houtkappers* and the police, and we didn't expect or need their help. We noticed, however, that Izak had managed to get off one shot before he died, and we wondered where it had gone. There was no sign of any bigfoot blood at the spot, but we did find a few drops nearby, and the next people to see the previously undamaged animal noticed both the broken tusk and the clean, round bullethole in his left ear!"

THE whole idea of "rogue" elephants is under review.

In Kipling's day, some were even believed to be "maneaters." One solitary male near Mandla in the Central Provinces of India in the early 1870s killed and dismembered a number of people and was seen, on several occasions, walking off with a loose arm or leg in his mouth. In 1872, the American hunter George Sanderson traveled to another village near Mysore where a second ferocious elephant had taken possession of eight miles of road, harassing and chasing anyone who passed by. It was safe to travel there only in large parties, beating tom-toms and sounding horns. Anyone on his own ran the risk of being knocked down and kneeled on while the crazed bull tore his arms and legs from their sockets and threw them some distance away. When Sanderson finally succeeded in killing this elephant, he found an abscess as large as a football under his tail.

Most homicidal elephants prove, in the end, to have been shot at and wounded, or to be suffering from giant toothaches. Their reputation as "rogues" seems to derive from pain or injury which drives them to extreme pathological behavior about as often as human beings become criminally insane.

Joyce Poole in Kenya puts all such madness down to sexual intoxication. During sexual intoxication, male elephants of either genus secrete a viscous liquid which runs in a dark line down the cheek from the opening of a swollen temporal gland just behind the eye. This stain also marks a period of heightened aggression, beginning in the "retirement" area where bulls usually gather away from the herd of cows and calves. This male society is a loose one. Bulls that do associate closely tend to be from the same families, but even relatives avoid each other when any of them are "in musth."

At such times, adult bulls pace to and fro, grumbling and picking fights, worrying the glands with their trunks, marking trees, wallowing in their own urine, and charging everything that moves. Any two bulls in musth at the same time clash violently in battles that can lead to injury and death, but the victor does get to join the females and mate with as many as he can.

Any human intruding on this sequence is at risk, even those like Joyce Poole and Cynthia Moss who have worked with the Amboseli elephants for fifteen years or more and know, and are known by, all of them. Testosterone rules, and can only be turned off after defeat by a higher-ranking musth male. Then the madness subsides, intoxication passes and the "rogue" reforms and goes off on his own or to join the other bulls in temporary retirement.

Everything that has been learned about elephant society in recent years, however, suggests very strongly that it would be wrong to assume that any elephant on its own is necessarily "solitary." The "herd" is a far looser concept than we imagined, and it seems that there is seldom a moment when even an old male who seems to be a loner is not in fact in some kind of contact with other males or with members of the groups of females and calves.

A totally isolated elephant is not an elephant at all and is likely to be more than a little out of character.

"*SOME* bigfeet carry grudges," insisted Kroos.

"After his battle with the bulldozer, this bigfoot became known as *Aftand*—'Lost Tooth'—and everyone in the forest went in fear of a meeting with him. People were afraid to go out at all after dark. They knew what had happened to my brother, and Aftand knew and never forgot who had shot at him.

"There was even talk about a hunting party to avenge Izak, but I spoke against that. Aftand was just protecting what was left of his herd and his home. I don't blame him, but he seems to have taken a strong dislike to me. I have had to run from him on several occasions, and today, I'm sorry to say, he deliberately hunted me down. Maybe I smell like my brother, perhaps we have a family flavor, but I know he used our interest in that cow to set up an ambush for us. It almost worked. I never had any hint of his presence until the very last moment, and then it was only a sudden coolness of the skin, some-thing I have learned to recognize as a danger signal. I should have known better, I should never have put your life at risk in this way! But I felt it was important for you to see a bigfoot for yourself. . . ."

I assured him that I wouldn't have missed this morning for the world. It is easy to be brave after the event, but I was actually exhil-arated by our elephant hunt in reverse, and there was so much more I wanted to know, but I had to tread carefully.

"Kroos," I ventured, "there is something I don't understand. You and your father and your father's father were all *houtkappers*. The forest was all you knew, but you only knew part of that. Woodcutting was your life. You knew what needed to be known to live that life, and not much more. I suspect that there was very little curiosity amongst your family about the details of nature around you, or about anything in the outside world, so . . ."

I paused, and he filled in the gap for me: "So how did I get interested?" I nodded.

"I met someone when I was young. A *rondloper*. You would be surprised at the number of people there are who wander in the forests, never settling down, living like phantoms that are seldom seen. He was not from here, and yet he was not an *uitlander*—an outsider. Quite the opposite, he seemed to belong here more than I did. He was full of enthusiasm and knowledge. We used to walk together on bigfoot trails, and it was through his eyes that I really learned to see.

"There was never a better tracker. He could look at tiny marks in river sand and tell you if the spider who made them was pregnant. On one occasion, I saw him track a porcupine on a paved road! He was filled with the pleasure of things, taking delight in the sort of detail nobody else could even see. He worked magic for me and changed my life forever, but there was no one I could tell. My family would never have understood. I couldn't even bring him home, because he wasn't like us. I was just a kid of sixteen and he was black. . . ."

Kroos paused with the faraway look that is part of remembering things of long ago. Then he seemed to come to a decision, and turning toward me he said very quietly:

"His name was !Kamma."

THE name hit me like a wall, but I wasn't completely surprised. For the last three years I had thought about that enigmatic Khoi person a great deal and had the feeling I would hear of him again.

Kroos watched the play of emotions in my face, and when these moved from astonishment to acceptance, he nodded and said: "I thought so. You knew him too!"

I had to think about that. The !Kamma I knew was of indeterminate age, but certainly older than I was. A lot older. Kroos was in his late sixties, so at least fifty years had passed since *his* meeting with the strange man. Could it be the same person? Was the !Kamma I knew older than Kroos? Could he have been in his eighties when we took him home to the hut? Did the arithmetic fit?

Yes, possibly. The Khoi and the San are famous for being ageless, for looking middle-aged for most of their lives. But I wasn't totally satisfied with this theory. Something was still missing. . . .

"Kroos," I asked, "how many bigfeet are here? How many have you seen?"

Kroos smiled gently and replied: "Everyone wants to know this. Always it seems to be about numbers. How old are you? How far is it? How much is it? These are not the important questions. These are all unnatural things, measurements we make up to satisfy our busy minds for a moment. You are as old as you feel; it is as long as it takes; and price has nothing to do with real value. The only measure that means anything to bigfeet is this—are there enough of us to be a family, a herd. Anything less is a disaster."

He was aware this sounded more like a reprimand than an answer and immediately softened his reply. "You and I today have seen two bigfeet. Aftand and the cow. She is the one who lost calves in 1942 and 1937, and is still angry. Then there is a young bull with hairy ears and a naked tail. He is very quiet. And another almost full-grown bull with a broken tusk, like Aftand, and also very suspicious of people. We call him Booytjie—'Little Man'. And a cow no one else has ever seen clearly. She stays with her calf in the deepest forest and always fades away. They call her Spook—'Ghost'—and her calf is Spooktjie—'Little Ghost.'"

He counted on his fingers: "That is six. But I know of another young couple with a calf that keep to the old forest at Lelievlei, and I have seen tracks of at least one more adult bull with feet so big they must be more than five feet around. Double that and you get his height. There's a measurement for you!"

He grinned at me as I made my own calculation. "That's ten," I said. "Is it enough?"

"Probably not," he acknowledged. "There are still those who shoot at them, even amongst the foresters themselves. People who shoot at anything that moves. But even so, there have been ten or twelve bigfeet in the forest ever since that madman came in 1920."

"Did you see him? Did you know Pretorius?" I asked.

"Oh yes. I was just married and needed the work, so I joined the beaters that day, and have regretted it ever since. It was a bloody mess. I was ashamed to have been part of it and never stayed to collect my pay. Pretorius was a man with death at his back. You could almost see the shadow over him. I carried part of that darkness away with me, and it nearly claimed me too on a day I walked through Moordlaagte—'Murder Hollow'—feeling desperate. All that saved me was the sight, for the second time in my life, of the White Elephant!"

THE cult of the white elephant goes back at least to the twelfth century B.C., but reaches its peak later in Thailand, where the rulers once bore the title Phra Chao Chang Phuk—"King of the White

Elephant." As late as the nineteenth century, Anna Leonowens, whose residence at the court of Siam led to *The King and I*, recorded how the discovery of a white elephant had to be reported to the capital immediately and the animal escorted there with care, prayer, and sumptuous entertainment, carried the last part of the journey down the Meinam River in a floating palace, curtained in crimson, thatched with flowers, fed on sugarcane and perfumed water, all presented on trays of gold. On arrival in Bangkok, the chosen elephant was housed in a magnificent pavilion, bejeweled and robed at the center of its own court of officers, musicians, attendants, and slaves. And when it died, probably of excess, the entire nation would go into mourning, which lasted until the elephant's brain and heart had been cremated and the rest of the body, laid on a bier and accompanied by dirges, was floated downstream and thrown into the Gulf of Siam.

White elephants in Burma and Cambodia were valued as rainmakers and oracles, every detail of their behavior scrutinized for omens that could alter affairs of state or lead to preparations for war being discreetly abandoned. So high was the value placed on truly white elephants that semi-albinos of a light beige color with blue eyes were eagerly accepted. There were even scandalous occasions on which elephants that had been painted white or in some way bleached were briefly enthroned.

The cult spread to China, Java, and Bali in dilute form and seems even to have taken root in Abyssinia. There are occasional images of white elephants on the rocks of the Sahara, amongst the masques of Mali, on the terra-cottas of northern Nigeria, decorating the palaces of Yoruba leaders on the Niger, as part of Ashanti folklore on the Gold Coast, as symbols used by elephant societies of the Cameroon grasslands, and in wall paintings in the Congo Basin. But there is little south of the equator until the vivid rock paintings of the San—whose isolation and Stone Age origins suggest a separate and parallel development of an animism that endows elephants, and other animals, with qualities that supersede the biological.

"HE isn't white, of course," said Kroos. "Any more than you are. Nor pink like the English, but more golden, like the fine, smooth color of finished yellowwood. He looks as though he has been freshly polished."

That sounded familiar to me.

Kroos continued: "But he is big. The largest bigfoot I have ever seen, with tusks that almost touch the ground. And yet he holds his great head high as though he doesn't have to carry what looks like three hundred pounds of ivory under his upper lip. I was just on the edge of the Garden of Eden, not far from that other big *kalander*, with my head hanging low, when something, it wasn't a sound or a movement, made me look up and beyond my own concerns. And there he was again, in the shade, standing tall as though he owned the forest. He did. He was magnificent, the true King of the Beasts. Forget your lions and tigers, this animal was imperial. He had an inner glow!"

I nodded. This was precisely how Owl and Starbuck and I had felt.

"I don't know how long I saw him that time," said Kroos. "Minutes maybe, but it was just like the first time. I couldn't move. I could scarcely breathe. And I don't know where he went. He just faded away and I was left feeling reborn. My black cloud had vanished with him and I felt like singing out loud. It seemed to me that any world, any place, that contained such a miracle was more than a match for the Pretoriuses!"

Just thinking about the event had left a bright light in his eyes, and his account put new hope in my heart.

Three years after my two brief sightings of the great white male, I had begun to question my memory of the elephant and to doubt its existence, but what Kroos had just told me revived the certainty, the excitement, and the awe I had felt at the time. I had smelled that animal and seen the color of his eyes!

I pressed Kroos for more information. "When did you first see him?"

"In the time of !Kamma," he replied. "I was just sixteen, a little like you, very full of myself, flexing my muscles, but not quite sure what to do with my mind. I had a strong sense of a gap in my life, a lack of information about the outside world. As *houtkappers'* children, none of us had any proper schooling. Some could read a little, but there was no access to books other than the Bible in Afrikaans.

"Then I met !Kamma. I was strolling through the forest on a Sunday. We never worked on the Sabbath, and I was just walking along thinking about nothing in particular when he stepped out from behind a fallen tree.

"*Jislaik!* I was too astonished to be afraid, and even though he was almost naked, he was so composed I found him interesting. We just stood looking at each other, and it was he who broke the silence. He said something in his funny language and beckoned me to follow. I did, and we pushed our way through the undergrowth, following no sign I could recognize. I realized eventually that he was so quick-sighted he was following bees in the air, watching to see which way they flew, working out where the hive must be. He led me directly to it in a hollow tree, where, together, we managed to break out a comb without getting stung too badly. The bees didn't seem to bother him at all. They gave up part of their hoard quite cheerfully, and we just sat on a log together and enjoyed the *dini*—that's what he called honey—laughing at the luxury and stickiness of it all!

"We met every Sunday after that, and he taught me how to track and how to speak some of his language. Did you know that *gogga*, meaning 'insect,' *dagga*—'marijuana'—and *aitsa*—'well-I-never'— are all Khoi words? Those and wonderful words like *hii*, which just means 'come' if you say it quickly, but if you drag it out a little describes a whole scene. Then it means 'poking a stick into a burrow to find out if the animal who made it is still there'!"

Kroos laughed. "I also taught him some of my language, a few words which he picked up very quickly, but just as we were beginning to make real progress, he vanished, as suddenly as he had appeared. I went out to our usual meeting place one Sunday and waited there for hours, but he never showed up. I was just about to give up and go home for dinner when I saw a movement beyond the fallen tree where we had first met. I went over to have a look, expecting to catch him playing one of his strange games, but in the clearing beyond stood the White Elephant!

"I was very scared at first. *Bangbroek!* There is a story amongst *houtkappers* here in Knysna about a ghostly white elephant that appears just before the death of someone important. To see it is said to be very unlucky. The death could be your own! Most sightings are in Phantom Pass on the way to George, where people also claim to have seen a headless rider on a pale horse. I never paid much attention to the tales, but this extraordinary bigfoot was so beautiful that I soon lost my fear and became totally absorbed by it. Then it was gone and I felt a strange mixture of sadness and joy. I didn't know whether to laugh or to cry, so I did neither, but it was very clear to me that this bigfoot was important and somehow connected with !Kamma, because I never saw him again."

Kroos stopped talking and gave me the space to think about what he had said. It sounded right to me. I too had felt that the little brown man and the big white animal were involved in some way, but had been unable to understand how. There was nothing in my experience to suggest any sensible explanation, and what Kroos said next didn't help at all. . . .

"Do you know what *!kamma* means in the language of the Khoi?"

I shook my head.

"I do," he said. "I thought at first it was *gamma*, which means 'lion,' but when I sorted out all the click sounds, I realized that I was not putting my tongue in the right place. His name was !Kamma with a tsk sound at the front—and that means 'a dream' or 'a dreamer'!"

MY head spun. Could this be true? Was the whole experience nothing more than a dream? Were Kroos and I caught up in some kind of vision?

I found it hard to believe. My experience had been shared by a group of young boys with nothing in our background to predispose us to such flights of fancy. We had bonded in the hut and had become, while the Strandloper Club lasted, more than the sum of our unpretentious parts, but even such new awareness fell far short of the sophistication required to conjure up an experience that included lessons in aboriginal astronomy and linguistics!

And Kroos, from a totally different culture and another generation, had just provided me with extraordinary corroboration of that experience, including details it would be hard to fabricate or stumble upon by chance, when all he and I had in common was curiosity, a preoccupation with elephants, and time spent in the same piece of Cape coastal forest.

Was that enough to share an almost identical dream? Was I missing something?

Perhaps so. In the last few years, information has surfaced about the Cape Coast that makes it every bit as seminal and magical as the Great Rift Valley—and that, heaven knows, has been the source of some of the most imaginative and largely unsubstantiated speculation in the history of science.

For half a century, thanks mostly to the Leakey family, we have become accumstomed to a version of the human family tree that appears to be firmly planted in East Africa. There is little doubt that many of our early triumphs took place there and were recorded in the fossil memory of Olduvai, Koobi Fora, and Hadar. But that narrow focus doesn't give sufficient weight to an equally long line of discoveries in the limestone caves of Swartkrans, Sterkfontein, and Kromdraai in South Africa, where a different kind of tree is being resurrected. And even this fails to give due weight to the possibility that none of the fossils from either area is the direct ancestor of living humans. The "missing link" may lie instead much further south—right on the Cape Coast!

PALEOANTHROPOLOGIST Lee Burger believes that the real answer lies in the ever-moving, largely unmapped fossil fields of the Coastal Cape. This is where the 500,000-year-old skullcap of Saldanha Man was discovered in 1953, showing a sudden increase in brain size and a shift in dentition and facial architecture that hints very strongly at the modern human form.

And yet it isn't even mentioned in many of the major publications of those whose reputations rest on more northerly sites.

To less-biased eyes, it seems obvious that Saldanha Man represents an early form of archaic *Homo sapiens,* the first of our kind. Perhaps even the very first! A 1987 study of mitochondrial DNA—the part we inherit from our mothers only—traces our origins back about 300,000 years to an "Eve" who lived in Africa, suggesting that humans resulted from a local speciation event that had nothing to do with relatives already living in Europe or Asia. No mention was made of the exact homesite of this founding mother, but there is good evidence to suggest that it was on the Cape Coast.

On the shores of Langebaan Lagoon, just a few miles from the place where Saldanha Man was found, a small site has recently been excavated. It contains the fossil remains of more then two hundred species of animals, giving some idea of the wide biodiversity that existed here at the time. In 1993, Lee Burger found the first of several archaic human teeth near there among the remains of a hyena lair going back 300,000 years. And in 1996, he and geologist David Roberts uncovered three clearly human footprints preserved in a fossil dune on the coast, impressed there following a heavy rainstorm 117,000 years ago. Prints very like the small, neat ones !Kamma left on wet sea sand near the hut!

The Khoi and the San are our last vestige of a living link to the Stone Age. They were responsible for the first art in the world, and probably also the first burials, the first ritual use of red ocher, and the development of several other culturally modern forms of behavior. And they lived, as Saldanha Man lived, in the Cape crucible—the narrow strip of coast isolated from the rest of the world by a cold ocean and a high mountain barrier. It had a unique and exceptionally rich and diverse ecology which contained a whole floral kingdom. A good place to grow, out of the maelstrom of the rest of Africa, and to develop new strategies for survival before bursting out again in an expansion fueled by superior brainpower and modern cultural inventions. And amongst these pioneers, there was a woman who carried the genetic potential of us all—including a small brown goblin with a hearty laugh who goes by the name of !Kamma, the Dreamer, and appears in places with the kind of natural power that allows strange things to happen.

I REMAIN in two minds about !Kamma.

His presence fifty years ago is still so fresh in my mind that I can smell the *buchu* oil on his skin and see every wizened little wrinkle on his cheeks. I didn't dream him and I don't believe Kroos did either. Yet he taught me to speak rudimentary Khoi half a century after breaking honeycomb with Kroos, all without seeming to age by even a day. And it wouldn't surprise me to hear that he was seen by someone else last week leaning nonchalantly against the trunk of a yellowwood tree watching tourist traffic flow through Phantom Pass!

As far as I am concerned, !Kamma is more enigma than dream. There is little I can do to attest to his existence, and I surrender any further judgment of or about him, but I continue to wonder about his elephant.

For a start, I am impressed by the power of the white elephant as an idea. There may never have been a purely white elephant anywhere, but in Asia local leaders have adopted the idea, identifying themselves with the power and the purity of a rare and intelligent animal. They were quick too to extend this exclusivity to include others more powerful still than themselves. A cousin of the king of Siam, visiting the English court in the nineteenth century, reported back on his impression of Queen Victoria:

"She is of commanding appearance. One cannot fail to see that she is of illustrious birth, descended from noble and powerful rulers of the earth. She has the eyes, complexion, and, above all, the bearing of a beautiful, majestic white she elephant."

She was not amused.

In South Africa, the woodcutters of Knysna were a small, tightly knit society in a hostile world. A group in danger of being marginalized by their own kind and forced instead into being identified with other poor people of a darker hue. So they too adopted a pale legend, a mysterious white elephant that carried all the signs appropriate to their situation. Warning each other of the grave danger of becoming too deeply involved with nature.

The white elephant, in either hemisphere, exists as an entity in folklore. It validates a local culture, justifying its rituals and institutions, and defending the authority of those who perform and observe them. It expresses social approval for those who conform, and warns of dire consequences for those who do not. But at the same time, the same idea can also have the opposite effect, exercising its potency without prejudice. For people like Kroos, it can provide a lifeline by making the unusual acceptable, building bridges to a new world that could otherwise be frightening. So the white elephant as a cautionary tale, as a bogeyman, is transformed into an instrument for change. Even for a group of white kids playing Strandlopers!

IT may also be a lot more than that.

Everywhere in Africa, savanna elephants are in decline, threatened by hunting and habitat destruction. With each year that passes, their future seems less and less secure, and conservation efforts are shifting instead to a more elusive from that never left the tropical rain forests. This still exists in relatively large numbers in the Congo Basin and in Cameroon.

Forest elephants tend to be smaller, with narrower heads, more rounded ears, and shorter, thinner, denser tusks that point straight down. All adaptations are designed to make it easier for them to move through dense vegetation, and now that DNA studies have shown that there are also significant genetic differences between forest and savanna populations, it has been suggested that the forest form of African elaphant ought even to be considered as a separate species–*Loxodonta cyclotis.*

As the savanna itself is a relatively new habitat in Africa (there was none before the Miocene), it seems likely that the ancestors of all African elephants were forest dwellers. The savanna itself was partly a product of a drier climate, but also in good part elephant-made, produced and maintained by forest elephants practicing the forest habit of knocking trees down to get at the leaves and fruit. In the forest that makes sense, and also opens up the canopy to create sunlit glades where second growth, much to the elephants taste, can thrive. Once out on the open savanna, there was no limit to body height, ear shape, or tusk size, so all these features changed, producing elephants that were larger, heavier, with bigger ears, longer tusks, and a greater difference in size between the sexes. In large groups, out of the forest, the bigger the bulls became, the greater was their sexual success.

There were other changes in social behavior. The groups of forest elephants are still small and far more widely spaced. Food and water in the forest are generally easier to find and not so seasonal, avoiding any need for elephants there to collect in large groups around short-lived resources. And the relative scarcity of large predators in the forest allows young elephants to be far more independent, straying from their parents in ways that would soon prove fatal on the savanna. Out there, safety lies in large groups led by big adults capable of defending whole nurseries of calves.

Elephants in the Addo are clearly savanna animals that have once again adopted typical forest strategies—showing less bulk, smaller tusks, and more rounded ears. All characters that make sense in that succulent wilderness, but ones that have been revived surprisingly quickly, plucked out of the ancestral gene pool to be used again with what, in the usual evolutionary time frame, could be described as indecent haste.

The Knysna elephants show no such obvious changes. They appear to be unrepentant savanna animals whose traditional range has been modified, mainly in the last few centuries, by humans who confine them now to the relative safety of shrinkingly small forest retreats. Given half a chance, they readily and happily take the sun and the opportunity to graze in the open whenever this seems safe to do. But each herd, in the Knysna and the Addo, has clearly made psychological adjustments that reflect not only recent persecution but the advantages of long residence in the crucible of the Cape. These are sophisticated elephants, very quick to learn and use new tricks, and never slow to reach back into their gene pools for old solutions to perennial problems.

FIVE million years ago, at the end of the Miocene, the climate of the Coastal Cape was warmer, wetter, and more tropical. Sea levels were falling and the land was covered in marshes and forests. There were sabre-toothed cats, bear-dogs, giant pigs, short-necked giraffes, and deerlike animals with permanent antlers. There were also elephants of several experimental kinds.

These included strange primeval elephants with four tusks, elephants more like mammoths than loxodonts, and one true elephant that may have been the earliest member of its family anywhere. This species could have been the direct ancestor of the southern stock that survives now only at the Addo, thanks to last-minute concern and a stout fence, and at Knysna, where it clings to life despite human intervention and because of its astonishing adaptability.

Recent paleontological finds on the Cape Coast have also included a gomphothere—one of the "beasts that are bolted together" and are believed to have been ancestral to mammoths, mastodons, and modern elephants. This fossil is called *Anancus*, and the exciting thing about it is that it is described as tall and high-browed, with long front legs and extraordinary tusks, of great length and girth, very straight and almost meeting near the ground!

Sounds familiar, doesn't it? It is a fossil, of course, and carries no hint of the color and condition of its hide, but I would be willing to bet that in the shade of a forest glade, this giant male would have had the look of patinated bronze, with skin the color of old ivory. I would be reluctant to bet against the possibility of a Knysna elephant, under severe selection pressure and the threat of extinction, reaching back to the Miocene for genes that could, even at this last gasp, be reactivated to save the day.

Back in 1955, I knew little of evolution and nothing of genetics. I was not quite sixteen and needed a far broader base of knowledge to come to any useful conclusion about elusive elephants and aboriginal man. My eyes and mind were saturated with the sights and sounds of the coastal forest, and I was content to leave interpretation of it all until later.

It was time, anyway, to take leave and take up my promised place in a university further north. . . .

CHAPTER SIX

Knowing the Elephant

There is mystery behind that masked gray visage,
an ancient life force, delicate and mighty, awesome and
enchanted, commanding the silence ordinarily reserved
for mountain peaks, great fires and the sea.
—PETER MATTHIESSEN in *The Tree Where Man Was Born*, 1972

I HAD decided not to go into medicine. I needed more than one species in my life and slipped from the medical stream at the University of the Witwatersrand into pure biology, but one thing kept drawing me back to the anatomy department.

His name was Raymond Arthur Dart. An Australian exile, drafted to Johannesburg in 1923 to help bring higher education to what was still little more than a mining town. What he found there was a group of ramshackle tin-roofed huts in the shadow of the main jail, but what he worked there was magic. Within two years, this already-balding thirty-year-old academic firebrand had not only set up a flourishing medical school but made one of the most seminal discoveries in the history of anthropology.

It was a classic case of the "prepared mind." Dart needed fossils for his classes on comparative anatomy and had persuaded a quarryman in the northern Cape to send him anything interesting from the local limestone works. He was hoping for any primate, perhaps an extinct species of baboon, but what turned up in one box of oddities was a tiny fossil face with a high forehead and delicate cheekbones. An exquisite thing, with all its teeth intact, too small to be a man, but definitely not a monkey. So Dart called it *Australopithecus africanus*—"Southern Ape of Africa"—and, in a paper published in 1925, announced that Charles Darwin was right: "Our early progenitors lived on the African continent."

This shattering news from an enthusiastic but unknown anatomist in the wrong part of the world was dismissed out of hand by the northern establishment as nothing more than a "juvenile ape." Dart himself was chastised, not just for rushing into print, but for the spurious sin of having mixed Latin with Greek in naming it *Australopithecus*. Faced with one of science's greatest discoveries, the experts quibbled about etymology!

The fossil from Taungs was shelved for more than twenty years, championed only by another remarkable and unorthodox man. Robert Broom was a Scottish physician working in small towns in the Karoo desert, because a practice there kept him close to another kind of fossil. In his spare time, he had already made himself the world authority on mammal-like reptiles, publishing 250 papers describing more than two hundred new species. His energy and enthusiasm were legendary, and after paying homage to Dart's find in Johannesburg, he dropped his reptiles and his patients and, at the age of seventy, set out to vindicate Dart by finding an adult of the same species.

He did just that. By 1947, he had discovered a whole series of hominids in the Transvaal, more than enough to convince the doubters gathered in Nairobi for the First African Prehistory Conference that Africa was indeed the Cradle of Man.

By the time I got to Johannesburg, Broom was dead at eighty-five, buried in his beloved Karoo, wearing his usual dark suit, wing collar, and butterfly tie. Dart himself was sixty-four, no longer able to swing from the hot-water pipes in his lecture room in imitation of a brachiating gibbon, but still raising Cain, going well beyond the visible evidence, following intuitive trails into human prehistory, conjuring up vivid and enthralling pictures of our ancestors.

I loved his lectures and persuaded him to let me work, free and in my spare time, on a new collection of bones he had amassed from a cave called Makapansgat. Many of these were blackened in a way that suggested the use of fire and prompted Dart to call the site the Cave of Hearths and those hominids found there *Australopithecus prometheus.*

I found the sheer volume of bones overwhelming. Row upon row of antelope and pig mandibles, femurs, loose teeth, and horn cores covered lines of trestle tables in an old army hut on the campus. There were tens of thousands of them, some arranged on shelves, some overflowing into wooden boxes on the floor, all neatly numbered and waiting for a sorcerer to bring them back to life.

As a sorcerer's apprentice, I was not very useful. For me, the bones were mute. I couldn't find a convincing pattern in them, but I hung on anyway, waiting for the times when Dart himself came through, bristling with energy and new ideas. His vitality seemed to spill out over the fossils, jerking them back into life, endowing them with design and purpose, turning them into unquestionable cutters, scrapers, daggers, clubs, and probes. All the makings of a culture. To me Dart was the last of an epic breed, the sole survivor of a time of great scientific shamans, and I hung on his every word.

"I wish old Broom had seen this," he said one day. "These fossils are the final proof that our apemen walked upright, that they made and used tools and had the kind of intelligence and discrimination to acquire the power of speech!"

He was never slow to leap to great conclusions, a talent I admired, but what I really wanted was help with my own difficulty in coming to terms with strange elephants. There was no easy way to work my proboscids into our discussions, but his mention of Robert Broom opened the door. . . .

"I miss Broom," said Dart. "He was thirty years older than I and great fun. Did you know that he gave a series of lectures on evolution to the divinity students at Stellenbosch in 1905? The Boer War was barely over, but he packed the largest hall in the university. He had those sons of Calvinism sitting in the aisles and hanging from every window ledge twenty years before the Scopes Monkey Trial in Tennessee!"

Dart admired anyone who challenged orthodoxy. "Broom never stopped. He told me he was determined to wear out rather than rust out. He was eighty-five when he finished his four hundred and fiftieth publication. It was a giant monograph on all the South African apemen, and as he made his last correction to the manuscript, he put down his pen and said: 'There, now that is finished . . . and so am I.' He was dead by morning."

I asked if there was anything left unfinished, and Dart thought a moment and said: "Actually, yes. In addition to his medical degree, he later submitted a doctoral thesis to Glasgow University—and that was never published. It had to do with Jacobson's organ, which he claimed was the best anatomical guide to relationships amongst the vertebrate animals."

Dart let me mull over this for a moment and then finished on a mischievous note: "Broom even tried to persuade me that his fossil reptiles were our direct ancestors . . . lizard-men!" he harumphed.

I HAD never heard of Jacobson or his organ, but a visit to the library remedied that.

Ludwig Levin Jacobson, I discovered, was a Danish anatomist

who in 1811 described a pair of pits to be found in the palate of a number of animals, most notably in snakes. He didn't know what their function might be, but Broom did, near the end of that century. He had several ideas.

He found the same pits in the roof of the mouth in fossil reptiles from the Karoo, many of them more than 200 million years old. And said: "It would seem that the organ of Jacobson is the organ in the body that is least liable to become altered by change of habit. I can almost identify an animal by examining this organ and often tell of its affinities." He suggested that it was part of the sensory system, an aid to olfaction, a way in which snakes, for instance, could "taste" molecules by collecting them from the ground with their flickering tongues.

As a child, I had found and captured and examined enough snakes to be familiar with their forked tongues, and known that these were used for investigation of each other or potential food. The more strange an object was, the faster the tongue came into play, applying its forked tips to matching pits in the roof of its mouth. But it had never occurred to me that Jacobson's organ was so widespread. I found mention of it in papers on opossums, anteaters, bats, cats, and even a white whale—so what about elephants?

I asked Dart, and he was intrigued enough to suggest that we check it out, there and then; so he and I walked across to the Anatomy Museum to look at its elephant skull. It was that of an African elephant, full-grown, probably female, with no tusks, but good teeth in both jaws. And there, near the back of the palate, were the clearly visible marks of a pair of pits in the bone, about two inches apart!

Dart was delighted. He never failed to become excited about anything new and different, and wondered if we were looking at a functional organ. Did it work? And why was it back there, in the old reptilian position? Was the elephant more primitive than we realized? And how could it now be used? Elephant tongues are fleshy and well equipped with the sensory papillae responsible for taste. Elephants can be very fussy about their food. But the free part of the tongue is less than three inches long and could never reach back to the pits of Jacobson's organ.

Then, almost in unison, it occurred to both of us: "The trunk!" Elephants are always putting trunks into their own and other elephants' mouths. What better way of getting to know one another?

"And," I added, wide-eyed, "African elephants have the added advantage of having a trunk with *two* fingers on the tip—which just happen to be about two inches apart!"

THE organ of Jacobson is one of those forgotten body parts. There are passing mentions of it in medical and technical journals dedicated to comparative anatomy and olfactory physiology, where it tends to be dismissed as something vestigial, an anatomical ghost that makes a transitory appearance in the human embryo, vanishing well before birth.

It is easy to miss. In humans, the external evidence consists simply of a pair of tiny pits, one on either side of the nasal septum, half an inch or so above the nostril. These no linger sit on the palate, but with the rearrangement of our faces to allow for binocular vision, have migrated to a more convenient spot, right in the airstream that serves the mainline olfactory sense cells in the nasal cavity. And they still seem to work.

When Dart and I talked, hardly anyone believed in such a thing. Now, more than thirty years on, the organ has been rediscovered under the more clinical description "vomeronasal organ" and given its obligatory acronym—the VNO. But by any name, it is an exciting development—a new sense organ with an ability to detect chemical signals previously thought to be beyond the scope of human sensitivity. Tests with microelectrodes show that it responds mainly to a range of substances which have large molecules, but no consciously detectable odor. And it communicates, not with the new improved olfactory bulbs in the cortex of the brain, where we marshal what we know and can remember about particular odors, but with the limbic system in the back of the brain, where the basic emotions involved in sex and aggression still seem to be coordinated.

The consequences of having two such separate and parallel systems of odor detection, one conscious and the other unconscious, are just beginning to be investigated, but the initial evidence suggests that they cooperate in surprising ways to produce novel sensibilities not achievable by either system on its own.

In no mammal is the opening to Jacobson's organ obvious. It is not like a flared nostril, but tends to be tucked away, as ours is, somewhere on the edge of the airstream. In most hoofed animals it is sidelined in a nasopalatine canal, which runs from mouth to nose near the nostrils, leaving two channels through the bony palate that can be seen very clearly just behind the upper incisor teeth on any goat or deer skull. And to expose the organ deliberately, many ungulates have developed a special facial expression. It is known by the German term *flehmen* or flared face and consists of a curl in the upper lip, the sort of grimace we make when faced with a strong odor. It is very common in antelopes and horses, especially among males exposed to the urine of a female in estrus, and is accompanied by a thrown-back gesture of the head which is very conspicuous.

What is happening in such circumstances is that a contraction of the lip-raising muscles brings pressure to bear on the nasopalatine canal, and that exposes the opening to the duct of Jacobson's organ. The head-raising and head-wagging helps out by allowing fluids in the mouth to flow across the lower opening of the canal that leads to the organ. Elephants, however, are faced with a different problem.

THERE are advantages to being big, but all tall animals inevitably have to deal in some way with the problem of reaching the ground in order to eat or drink.

Giraffes have developed long necks and a strange foreleg straddle that looks somewhat inelegant. Hippos simply shortened all their legs. The elephant's massive head and its active life precluded either solution, but the slack seems to have been taken up by the very versatile trunk.

We assume from the existence of bony nostrils high on the skulls of ancestral elephants that these extinct forms had a trunk of some kind, just as modern elephants do, but there is no good way of telling how long it might have been. Reconstructions paint a convenient picture. They show trunks of gradually increasing length down through all the ages of elephant prehistory. But chances are that, the giant genetic decision to elongate and combine the nose and upper lip having been made, the full trunk may have followed very quickly. The advantages of having such a multipurpose organ are far too good to delay, and easy eating and drinking would have been only part of the benefits realized. There will also have been strong selection pressures in favor of better smell.

The height of elephants puts their olfactory sense cells a long way from the ground, well above the critical odor zone; but an elongated trunk solves the problem, putting nostrils back down there on the ground, where scents abound.

The fact that this is so, and that elephants find it useful, can be confirmed by watching any elephant for just a few minutes. The tip of the trunk is never still; it is in constant motion, moving in the direction of every stimulus, probing, checking, sampling both air and ground, subtly signaling an interaction before it even occurs. And newborn elephants come ready-equipped with everything they will need except experience.

Cynthia Moss describes baby elephants stepping on or falling over their unruly new trunks, finding they often get in the way. Some solve the problem by sucking the tip in the same way that a human sucks its thumb, but "the baby's trunk is its main medium of contact with the world around it." It is there despite the difficulties.

Smell is clearly as emotive for elephants as it is for us, and never more so than when sex is involved. Katy Payne tells of a bull elephant in musth moving amongst a herd of females: "He reaches out his trunk to test a pool of urine left by one of the females in the group that surrounds him. After him, several other large males extend their trunks in the same gesture. Each one sniffs, wrinkles his trunk, blinks his eyes, and lifts his trunk to the roof of his opened mouth where he shunts the inhaled smell of female urine to the vomeronasal organ, which enables him to evaluate the female's reproductive condition."

Someone is in breeding condition and the news is out, communicated by the largest Jacobson's organ in the world.

IN 1952, the Austrian zoologist Konrad Lorenz published *King Solomon's Ring*, a ground-breaking account of his work on jackdaws and the behavior of greylag geese, showing how each was programmed to pick up specific kinds of information that were important for survival.

I was excited by Lorenz's discussions of instinct and imprinting, and by the possibility of using this new science of ethology to interpret elephant behavior. So as soon as I graduated in 1958, I decided to leave South Africa and throw myself and my proboscid problems at his feet. Being a colonial son and part of a small society has its advantages. It never occurred to me, as it would to someone in a more structured larger pool, that one didn't just do that, descending unannounced on famous people. But when you don't know something is impossible . . .

Dart was all for it. He knew about Lorenz from his early publications on comparative anatomy in Vienna, and he waxed lyrical about the heroic tradition of passing from mysterious childhood to the great voyage which pits a budding hero against the necessary trials and tribulations that will make him a man. He actually said: "Go, my son. Go and return victorious!" And shed a tear. . . .

So I went to Westphalia and knocked on the door of the new Max Planck Institute for Behavior Physiology in Seewiesen. Lorenz was very kind. He listened to my stories about elephants and offered me the chance to join his growing group of young ethologists—studying tropical fish!

This wasn't quite what I had in mind, so I thanked him courteously and left to confront the Dutch zoologist Niko Tinbergen, who, in 1973, was to share the Nobel Prize with Lorenz for their joint work in establishing the science of animal behavior. Tinbergen had just moved from Leiden to Oxford University to organize a new research department, and didn't seem overly surprised to see me. I wondered later if Lorenz had put out a warning about crazy African students who wanted to work on elephants in Europe! Tinbergen was amused by my presumption—I was still only nineteen—and graciously suggested that he might be able to find a place in his department for another doctoral student, if I joined a team working on various aspects of the behavior of the black-headed gull!

How many zoologists does it take to study a gull? Lots, it turned out, but I was at least consoled by the thought that I was moving up the evolutionary tree from fish to birds! I thanked Tinbergen courteously and said I really needed to learn about mammals. He considered my predicament for a moment and said: "One of my students has just left to become Curator of Mammals at London Zoo. I suppose he might be able to supervise you there, and if he will, I would be happy to referee your thesis."

I discovered later what an incredibly generous gesture this was to an unknown young stranger. Fortune, it seems, does favor the bold. And I left for London with high hopes. . . .

DESMOND MORRIS was delighted with the idea. I was his first student, Tinbergen's sponsorship virtually guaranteed my registration at the University of London, and I soon discovered what an honor it was to work at the zoo.

London Zoo, or the Gardens of the Zoological Society of London, was founded under Royal Charter in 1826 "to further the advancement of Zoology and Animal Physiology and the introduction of new and curious subjects of the animal kingdom." This Victorian sentiment was still very much in evidence in the 1950s, and I wondered, to begin with, if I had come to the wrong place to learn about the behavior of mammals in the wild.

Far from it. I will always have my reservations about zoos in general, because no matter how hard they try, or how great the need to keep and breed rare animals may be, the captive situation will always be second-best. Nothing can replace the wild, particularly for highly social, active, intelligent, and easily bored animals like elephants. But I learned at London Zoo that an institution built around a learned society and a great library, involving scientists and technicians at every level of expertise, had a great deal to offer naturalists like myself.

Desmond taught me how to use the zoo as a living library, with a reference section dedicated to every class of animal. If you came across a problem involving mongooses, monkeys, or moths, all you had to do was stroll out into the gardens and look at a wide selection of species from every corner of the globe. They might not be demonstrating every aspect of their behavioral repertoire, but you could examine them at close quarters and, failing all else, find someone nearby who had seen them in the wild and could fill in the gaps in your knowledge.

The zoo was a magnet for every luminary in the business. Lectures, discussions, and seminars held there tended to overflow into the gardens, where you could bump into people like Louis Leakey, Bernhard Grzimek, and Jacques Cousteau just watching the giant panda or visiting penguins.

But one of the introductions I most treasured was to Desmond's former professor at Oxford, a gentle, erudite scholar named Alister Hardy. He started as a marine biologist, serving on expeditions to the Antarctic, working with whales and seals, exploring the origins of life in the water, following a liquid metaphor which led to an almost spiritual ecology he described in *The Living Stream.*

Hardy was one of those rare life scientists who believed that alongside the mechanics of heredity and natural selection there was some other organizing principle, something more psychic than physical—and he wasn't afraid to think about and talk about coincidence, the collective unconscious, and the possibility of telepathy. In 1975, he even published an influential argument entitled *The Biology of God,* which explored the natural history of spiritual experience.

He was a lovely man, and I particularly enjoyed his thoughts about elephants. As a biologist, he was fascinated by the yawning voids in our knowledge of the evolution of most orders of animals, and suspected that these were all too easily being filled with hopeful fossils that didn't really belong there. He called these "gods of the gaps" and suggested that it might be more profitable to look, not for missing links, but for missing influences. Our discussions kept coming back to worldwide legends and lore about the Flood, about a time when the world was covered with water. Hardy wondered if these were not so much residual memories of a deluge, but far older genetic impressions of a time when we were much more aquatic, following a return to the sea.

Dinosaurs did it. The carnivorous ancestors of whales and dolphins did it. Early bears and dogs took the plunge, becoming seals and otters. And several ancestral proboscids made the reentry, producing "sea cows"—the manatees and dugongs. "Take a close look at elephants," he advised. "Watch them swim; examine the webbing between their toes; remind yourself that without a trunk, elephant nostrils are on top of the head, like a whale's; look at the subcutaneous layer of fat beneath the skin and ask why they are almost hairless. Elephants are still happiest in the water—they only come ashore to feed!"

Later, Hardy was to extend these ideas about the sea as a force in evolution to their logical conclusion with the theory of the Aquatic Ape, but I never forgot his advice. It still feels right, for elephants and ourselves. Both of us went through a relatively recent aquatic phase that has set us aside from our nearest relatives, giving us the opportunity to grow bigger brains and the incentive to use them.

Meanwhile, back at the zoo, every day was a delight, filled with intellectual challenges posed by Desmond Morris, who woke up every morning with an entirely new idea. One that questioned all earlier thinking on a subject and promised to change our understanding of it forever. Whatever it was, he believed it totally, and we would spend the day exploring all the possible ramifications, only to discover on the following morning that Desmond had, without a blush, come up with another, even better, and totally contradictory idea. . . .

Desmond was always larger than life, filled with creative notions and good humor, generous with his time and his praise—the perfect supervisor. I completed my dissertation in the alloted three years, was approved by Niko Tinbergen in oral examination, and won my doctorate just as Desmond finished writing *The Naked Ape* and was forced to flee to a tax haven in Malta. I returned to South Africa to rebuild the Johannesburg Zoo.

That didn't get me any closer to solving my elephant problem, but I now had the knowledge I needed to approach it as a qualified ethologist, and the job offer was something a twenty-three-year-old naturalist would be a fool to turn down. Besides, that was where I met Delilah. . . .

THE Johannesburg Zoo was everything London Zoo was not. It was a municipal institution, short of cash, long on bureaucracy, and run by the Parks and Recreation Department. Which meant that the lawns were manicured, the flower beds lovely, but the animal quarters disastrous. I was the first professional zoologist to be employed there. Most of the staff were untrained, largely uninterested, and entirely white, working there only because no other department would have them.

It was an uphill struggle. Far too many pointless meetings, too much talk, and everything else in triplicate. Requisitions were a nightmare; it was always so much easier to say no rather than have to come and see problems for themselves "out at the zoo." We always seemed to be last on everyone's list of priorities. And then the only one who really cared, the man who had found me and hired me in London, left his post and we lost whatever clout we had, along with most of our budget. But then there was still Delilah. . . .

She was four years younger than I, a teenager, born in the bush, but having lived most of her life in Johannesburg. She was an orphan, the survivor of a massacre, but despite this background she was one of the sunniest, most consistently good-tempered individuals I have ever met. She was also truly beautiful, with long, thick eyelashes. And I was particularly fond of her trunk.

Delilah lived alone in a dark, damp, concrete-floored cage in what was euphemistically described as the Elephant House. More than half of her time was spent shackled indoors, chained to a ring in the floor that gave her the scope of just eight feet of chain. During the day, she had the "free run" of a compound half the size of a tennis court surrounded by girders of black steel bent out of shape by earlier, angrier denizens.

This was where I first met her, standing near her steel barrier, rocking gently in a way I had learned to recognize as one of the first signs of stress and mental illness. As I approached, she pushed out her trunk directly toward me in the gesture all elephants use on meeting strange or higher-ranking individuals. I knew, thanks to Desmond, that this was a "greeting-intention movement," one universally misinterpreted in zoos as "begging" and rewarded by offers of food, when what was really being sought was friendship. So I cupped the tip of her trunk in my hand and gently blew into it.

The result was extraordinary. She entwined my whole arm in her trunk, held it there as she breathed deeply several times, and then put the tip of her trunk in her mouth and sighed. I came a little closer and let her explore my face and neck freely until I could hear a soft growl of pure delight—the elephant equivalent of purring.

It was love at first sight, and I decided, then and there, that my first priority in this zoo would be a new elephant house and company, elephant company, for Delilah.

THAT took time, but as construction continued, I got the chance to get to know Delilah a great deal better.

To start with, her initial automatic, head-lowered, ears-flattened, swaying gesture of submission made me curse the early keepers who must have beaten her into obedience. But as we became better acquainted I was happy to see more confident approaches, raising her head, tucking her chin in, and lifting and flapping her ears—all in a short gallop to the fence, even before we had gone through the snaky business with our trunks.

I never fed her. That is not something elephants normally do for one another. I left that to her regular keeper, who by now was beginning to take a closer interest in her welfare. And eventually I decided it was time to go into the compound with her, alone. Just me and over eight thousand pounds of female elephant on a blind date.

To get into the outdoor area, I had to go through the store and the indoor area—the usual way keepers approached her, with all the usual sounds. But by the time I stepped out of the darkness into the sun, she was already taking unusual interest. She had heard, smelled, seen something other than her keeper and was *standing tall.* She flapped her ears and lifted her head very high, trunk spelling out the letter S in front of her head, the tip swiveling my way in full alert, a thin dribble of dark fluid on each cheek. "Oh-oh!" I thought. "This could go wrong. Have I miscalculated?"

She began to move toward me somewhat stiff-legged, trunk now hanging at a more acute angle, but still not showing the side-to-side head shake of outright threat. That would have sent me back indoors in a hurry. Then I heard the door close behind me, cutting off any retreat. The keeper obviously didn't want to be involved in any of this, or he wasn't very fond of me. Still she kept coming, keeping me guessing until the last moment, when she stopped right in front of me and very deliberately pressed the top of her trunk against my forehead so that I could feel a soft vibrant rumbling sound right through my body. She was leaning into me, purring something that sounded very much like "Hey! What took you so long?"

FOR a while, construction stopped altogether—something about the supply of cement—and I wondered what else I could do to keep

Delilah amused. I contemplated bringing back elephant rides. There were still a pair of brick ladders up near the War Memorial, gangways like those on airport aprons, where children once boarded a how-dah—a sort of saddle with seats—to be taken once around the swan lake for sixpence. It hadn't been used since an animal welfare organ-ization made a fuss, condemning it as demeaning to elephants. They were right, it is, but for elephants stuck in a cage it could have been a welcome change of pace. I was sure Delilah could be taught to wear the howdah and would enjoy the company, but the city fathers and their lawyers squashed the whole idea—and I got cement in a hurry.

In the meantime, and before zoo opening time, I took to walk-ing Delilah around myself. We used a form of bridle with a leather lead which both she and I pretended would keep her in line. It was never tested, for the simple reason that she really enjoyed walking around with me. She wasn't fond of monkeys or little creepy things like honey badgers and porcupines, so we avoided that part of the zoo and strolled instead between the paddocks of zebras, wilde-beests, and giraffes. These seemed familiar to her and she spent a lot of time with her trunk hanging over their fence, trying to remember where and when they had met. I'm not sure she ever did make the connection. She was only three years old when she was captured, and it can't have been more than just a faint memory of happy times with the herd.

Sometimes she let me grip her tail while she decided which way to go, trotting along, squeaking like a calf, reliving perhaps those times when her mother steered her with a firm trunkhold on her behind. And I could have sworn she found pleasure in this strange reversal of roles. But there was another day when this game nearly backfired.

Delilah must have heard lions before. There were several in the zoo and they roared almost every evening, giving people who lived in the crowded suburbs nearby a *frisson*, reminding them that, all immediate appearances to the contrary, they were still living in Africa. I am certain that lion smell had been part of her zoo experience for sixteen years and wouldn't normally disturb her. But I had forgotten, or was never told, that a new male lion—one said to look very like the extinct Cape lion—was being brought in that day and would be taken to the Lion Hill in our transport cage on wheels.

I even heard the tractor trailer coming our way, but this was such a normal part of zoo routine that I never thought twice about it until it was just twenty feet away and the lion flung himself at the bars with a deafening roar. That sound, anywhere nearby, is enough to turn your knees to water. In Delilah, it triggered an instinctive response. She whirled around and put herself between me and the lion, doing everything possible to assume a group defense all on her own. There were no signs of indecision, no trunk coiling or winding, no ear-touching or pulling up tufts of grass. Her tail stiffened in my hand, her back arched, her head shot up, and her ears spread out to their full extent, providing an awesome frontage of ten or twelve feet of gray anger studded with tusks and accompanied by an ear-splitting scream from her raised trunk.

Even from behind it was impressive. From the lion's side, it must have been absolutely terrifying. It took us two days to get him out of the traveling cage and an entire week before he dared to show his nose in the outdoor enclosure!

Delilah took it in her giant stride. For weeks afterward, whenever she thought no one was looking, I saw her replay her display, polishing some of the moves. And at the end of each silent rehearsal, she adopted that funny, loose-limbed sort of swagger that in the elephant world invariably indicates a large degree of self-satisfaction.

WHEN the domed buildings of the new elephant area were almost complete, we got word of a pair of young elephants who had survived a cull on the border with Botswana. I pulled a few strings, and within the week they were ours and on their way to Johannesburg.

The plan was to keep them in the old building next to Delilah so that they could get used to each other through the bars before they were all turned loose in their new home. Delilah's part of the original building was larger, better equipped for the two newcomers, so we moved her to the smaller older wing, which had not been used at all since her arrival.

She was reluctant to make the move and had to be led by hand into the wing, moving very slowly, step by step, hanging back as long as she could. The place had been spring-cleaned, scrubbed and furnished with fresh hay and water, but it was clear that she didn't like it. I stayed with her all the way, making encouraging noises, but that didn't help much. Maybe it was my accent. In the end, however, she settled down a little and we left her to it as I watched from behind the scenes.

She started sniffing first at the food and bedding, and then moved across to the other side of the indoor area, the tip of her trunk opening and closing, testing smells left and right, reaching out to its full extent as she got closer to the wall. Then the pattern changed; she began to concentrate on one spot in the corner, pausing, turning, hesitating, finally giving all her attention to that small area. She became very quiet, even tense, and stood right over the spot, giving it her undivided attention, so absorbed that even her trunk stopped moving. And she stayed that way, entranced, for minutes on end.

Everything about her demeanor reminded me of the young bull I had seen in the Addo investigating another elephant's skull. Eventually, Delilah shook herself out of the meditation and seemed to come to a decision. She went over to the hay pile, picked up a large sheaf with her trunk, and carried this across to the offending area. And she kept on transporting hay until the entire corner was completely concealed. Then she relaxed and seemed quite at home.

I called the keeper and showed him what she had done. It

didn't make any sense to him either until I asked how long it was since the wing had been used.

"*Gits*," he said. "Almost twenty years. This is where we kept the last African elephant. The one we had before Delilah arrived. . . ."

I asked what had happened to it.

"She became very sick and difficult and had to be kept shackled all the time. Until eventually the visiting vet said she would have to be put down. We shot her. . . ."

He paused and I could see that something had just occurred to him.

"*My God*," he said with his eyes wide. "That's where it happened, all those years ago. That's where she died. Right in that corner!"

EVERYONE connected with elephants has a similar story.

Joyce Poole: "I have observed a mother, her facial expression one I could recognize as grief, stand beside her stillborn baby for three days, and I have been deeply moved by the eerie silence of an elephant family as, for an hour, they fondled the bones of their matriarch."

Cynthia Moss: "Recently one of the big adult females in the population died of natural causes and we collected her jaw after a few weeks and brought it to the camp. Three days later her family happened to be passing through the camp and when they smelled the jaw they detoured from their path to inspect it. One individual stayed for a long time after the others had gone, repeatedly feeling and stroking the jaw and turning it with his foot and his trunk. He was the dead elephant's seven-year-old son, her youngest calf. I felt sure that he recognized it as his mother's."

Oria Douglas-Hamilton: "The tusks of the dead elephant excited immediate interest; they were picked up, mouthed, and passed on from elephant to elephant. . . . To begin with only the largest individuals would get near the skeleton, but the rest of the group now followed, many of them carrying pieces, which were dropped within about a hundred yards. . . . It was an uncanny sight to see those elephants walking away carrying bones as if in some necromantic rite."

And Sylvia Sikes: "If the female elephant is dead, they tear out branches and grass clumps from the surrounding vegetation and drop these on and around the carcass . . . then scrape soil toward the carcass and stand by, weaving restlessly from side to side."

The strange ritual of bone turning and dispersement is well documented. As is the apparently widespread response of burying the carcass. And it seems clear that elephants have no difficulty in recognizing the body parts of their own kin or the place of death of these, or strange elephants, even long after all obvious remains have been removed.

Ian Parker, who conducts culls, tells of herding elephants by aircraft toward a gun party on the ground, only to see these frightened animals suddenly change course and head instead for a distant and discolored patch of soil. There they stopped and made a thorough investigation with their trunks of the exact site of an earlier cull, before moving on together again to meet their own fate.

So Delilah's behavior was not aberrant. It was part of a well-developed, continent-wide pattern of action in which elephants recognize death and respond to it with rituals that result in dispersion or concealment of the remains, and seem to be deeply felt.

Is there perhaps something feline in this, a need to cover tracks? Very hard to do if you and the dead individual may each weigh as much as ten tons. There is also something rather humane in their concern, something very close to grief. When responding to the death of one of their kind, elephants become distinctly formal. They fall silent, moving with unusual decorum, observing what seem to be very solemn ceremonial acts. Last rites, perhaps?

Meanwhile, at the Johannesburg Zoo, the elephant area was opened, much to the delight of Delilah and her new friends, who spent a great deal of time there in constant contact, relishing being close to one another. We also completed a new big cat area, and a wolf wood, but then the building fund ran out completely, and I ran out of patience and decided to move on. . . .

MY dalliance with Delilah had upset a long-term plan to get into the field with elephants, but by the time I started looking for grants, Iain Douglas-Hamilton, a student of Niko Tinbergen's, had begun work on the ecology of elephants at Lake Manyara in Tanzania. So I joined BBC Television as a producer and presenter of science programs—and might be there still had I not, quite by accident, written a book titled *Supernature: A Natural History of the Supernatural.*

This was an attempt to make scientific sense of all the loose ends that lie, largely neglected, on the fringe of experience. It was astonishingly successful, spawning ten other books in the years that followed, leaving elephants behind. But, as it happens, what I learned about the paranormal began to make sense of some of the elephant mysteries, and, almost a decade after Delilah, I found myself drifting back to Knysna, where a lot, and nothing at all, had changed. There were still elephants in the forest and still very little agreement on how many were involved.

In 1969, Bruce Kinloch, former Chief Game Warden of Uganda and Tanganyika, did a ten-day survey. He expressed surprise that the numbers of elephants in Knysna had not changed in fifty years of "strict legal protection" and thought that there might be ten individuals. Later that same year, the local Wildlife Protection and Conservation Society commissioned another retired game warden from East Africa to make a far more thorough study.

For fifteen months, Nick Carter and two woodcutters from the Stroebel family crisscrossed the forest, walking trails, recording prints, examining dung, and taking a few precious photographs. Carter concluded that there were now eleven animals, including a newborn calf. He described and listed all the elephants he encountered, and I was glad to see Aftand and another male "with hairy ears" in his catalog of five bulls, four cows, and two calves. His report recommended that a fully protected and fenced area like that of the Addo was the only hope for the long-term survival of the herd.

This report and Nick Carter's recommendations were ignored. "My findings," he said with understandable disillusion, "burst upon the world with all the effect of a poached egg hitting the Indian Ocean." Nothing happened. The old official status quo of promising little and delivering even less was safely maintained. The Forestry Department continued to insist that it was fully capable of looking after the elephants without outside help. "Except for the grinding of my own teeth," said Carter, "all was quiet until April of 1971."

What happened then was awful. Carter describes it as "a tragedy with clowns." At the heart of it lay the traditional unwillingness of the Department of Water Affairs and Forestry to take proper responsibility for the elephants in its trust. Water and trees, as the department's full title suggests, are its business, and the elephants appeared to be a nuisance and a distraction. The department did, however, make one public concession to Carter and the conservation community—it promised to appoint a senior official to concern himself exclusively with the fauna of the indigenous forest, including the elephants. But less than a year later, a member of that very same department shot and killed the herd's patriarch—the great bull elephant, Aftand!

THE killer's name was Klaus von Gadow, a thirty-six-year-old forester and hunter from Germany who had been just dying to kill himself an elephant. His superiors were aware of the danger he represented. One even tried to contain this ambition by allowing him to make a collection of birds: to no avail. Half a century after Pretorius, von Gadow used the trivial incident of an elephant raid on a vegetable garden to justify drastic action. The damage amounted to 445 Rands, less than a hundred U.S. dollars, but on this basis alone von Gadow tracked down the most conspicuous elephant, which was always Aftand, and opened fire because "the elephant had made an annoyed movement."

Aftand, wounded in the forehead, took refuge in a thicket, now a cause for real concern, likely to savage anyone who came too close. At this stage von Gadow felt compelled to tell his boss what he had done. The immediate response of Chief District Forest Officer Friedrich von Breitenbach was to worry, not about an injured elephant, but about publicity that might embarrass the department. He instructed von Gadow to go back and kill the elephant "in secret," which he did two days later. Then the two of them, in the best interests of the department, of course, cut off the trunk, one ear, one foot, and both tusks and, in a macabre travesty of the elephants' own funeral rites, covered the carcass with branches and foliage.

Two months later the department "discovered" the body again and announced in a press release news of "the sad death of one of the world's most southerly herd of elephants." They blamed the killing on a poacher's bullet, probably involving "coloured honey hunters." By now, however, too many people in the small forest community knew what was really going on. A police investigation was called for, the tusks were discovered buried on von Gadow's property, and he and von Breitenbach were arrested and charged with "destruction of forest produce and hunting in the state forest."

The trial took nine days. Everyone turned against everyone else, old enmities and intrigues were revived, and mud was slung in every direction. The department came out of it very badly and the magis-

trate dismissed the defense case as "a web of lies," but was forced
in the end to dismiss both of the accused on a technicality.

Because the two were state officials acting in their official
capacities, the ordinance against hunting without a permit did not
apply to them. And they could not be held responsible for damage
to the elephant, or any of its body parts, because Aftand was "forest
produce," He and all the surviving elephants were the property of
the Forestry Department, to do with as they pleased!

This was how things stood when I got back to Knysna in 1972.
As so often in the old South Africa, official interests were given
precedence over public concern. The evidence—tusks, an ear, a foot,
and a jawbone—were said to be lost in the bowels of a bureaucracy
from which not even the local museum could extract them. And the
skull, apparently deliberately defaced by von Gadow to hide the evidence of his shooting, seemed to have vanished altogether.

Little was left of the big bull with the broken tusk, except a few
fuzzy photographs of an elephant with wild eyes peering defiantly
over the forest undergrowth, and the memories of those who knew
him. Sadly, the one who perhaps knew him best and bore him the
least ill will was no longer available to tell the true story of the giant.

Kroos Arend died without having to witness the indignity of
Aftand's going, and before I could renew my acquaintance with
either of them. But I found solace in the extraordinary but somehow
totally appropriate coincidence that Kroos had died in his home on
Sunday, April 4, 1971—just a few miles away and a few hours after
Aftand fell bleeding to the forest floor.

I WAS thirty-three years old by now, a published writer with
influential friends abroad, but this meant little in a South Africa
where "surplus black people" were being moved by force to poverty-

stricken reserves and Nelson Mandela was in just the seventh of his twenty-seven long years of detention.

The best I could do was to pay my respects to Kroos Arend, who, as I left seventeen years earlier, had said goodbye with the words "Seek the questions with no answers; for they are the only serious ones!"

That hadn't made a great deal of sense to me then, but as time went by and I began to find such questions in my path, I realized that the only truly serious questions are the ones asked by children in innocence. But by that time I was beginning to grow up and lose the necessary naïveté. . . .

So I went to see the Arend family, who, instead of burying Kroos in the town cemetery on the edge of the lagoon, had chosen to take him, secretly and after dark, out into the forest at Kruisfontein— "Spring of the Cross"—where they buried him in the same ground that had absorbed Aftand's dying blood.

The *houtkappers*, of course, learned of the circumstances of Altand's death long before it became public knowledge and were able to hold their funeral ceremony and Aftand's wake without official interference. I wished I could have been with them, but a year later the best I could do was to walk the five miles out of the village past the forest station toward Brackenhill Falls, from where I had no difficulty finding the killing ground. There were still truck tracks and disturbed areas on the forest floor, all leading to a ravine half a mile off the road. This was where the young blond forester, described by one of his seniors as "psychologically difficult material," came with a Mannlicher 9.5mm rifle to finish off a job he had started so badly two days before. The first long-awaited shooting must have been a high moment for him, an easy shot at a browsing elephant out in the open. This follow-up, under orders, up against a wounded bull at bay in dense undergrowth, was something else altogether. He could die here.

As it happened, it was Aftand who died, probably because he was already near death and easily dispatched. I like to think that van

Gadow would not have had a chance against an Aftand with all his awesome powers still intact.

I climbed down to where the carcass had been found. There amongst the rocks, even a year later, there was still the smell of death. Von Gadow will have known it, and felt it I hoped, as *Angstgeruch*, something that raises heart rate, blood pressure, and blood sugar, contracting the surface of the skin, widening the pupils, and making hair stand on end. It was enough to make me look, covertly, over my shoulder. I felt dry-mouthed and distinctly uneasy, but I was there for a noble reason. I had been told that Kroos was buried deep, in a rocky cleft at the base of a yellowwood tree just twenty feet from what little remained of Aftand. The family had marked the spot with a small gift—a piece of quar, aromatic hardwood of the gardenia family, carefully carved into a wagon-wheel spoke—the speciality of the *houtkappers* in the Arend family.

I found it easily enough, driven into a crack in the cliff, but it was almost impossible to recognize the rest of the cleft. It had been entirely obliterated, covered to a depth of six feet with a dense pile of sticks, branches, and loose pieces of timber; and all around were the great footprints of several elephants. They had not only found Kroos, but honored him with the ritual which marks the concern and respect they display for their own dead!

There was very little I could add to that, except a whispered "*Totsiens*"—till we meet again.

ZOOLOGIST Ivan Sanderson tells of a young elephant called Sadie, one of eight in a circus in Missouri. The group was being trained for an upcoming performance, and Sadie, the youngest, tried in vain to master the complex routines, until it all overwhelmed her and she fled the ring. Twice the trainers brought her back and chastised her, but on the third occasion she simply gave up, sank to her knees, and then lay down on her side, weeping. "She lay there," said one of the horrified trainers, "tears streaming down her face, sobs racking her huge body, like a child."

I know that in addition to their two protective eyelids, elephants have a third clear nictitating membrane that sweeps horizontally across the eyeball, lubricated by the Harderian gland. The secretion from this gland differs slightly from that of our lachrymal glands, but when there is enough of it, something very like tears trickles from the corner of an elephant's eyes and runs down its cheeks. And as this tends to happen when the animal is tired, sick, or emotionally disturbed, I see no reason not to conclude that elephants weep.

I have seen a zoo elephant shackled on its own do just that, and it is impossible not to be deeply moved. The least we can do in the circumstances is to allow that elephants are capable of feeling disturbed and of showing great concern. There is no other way of describing what happens when they gather around a dead herd member, playing their trunks over the fallen animal, touching its tusks, sniffing at a wound perhaps, and doing so in utter silence. Their whole comportment changes, there is none of the usual rumbling or pacing or scratching and scraping. They just look forlorn. They too appear to be deeply moved, and to deny them this capacity seems churlish and absurd.

The Knysna forest after the death of Aftand seemed different in just that way. It had always been quiet, a place of fleeting sounds and smells, but now it seemed preternaturally still. Respectful, I thought, or in a state of shock. The elephants never gathered together anymore; nobody had seen a herd since Pretorius shattered the silence fifty years before with his guns. But there seemed to be a kind of communion taking place, as though the scattered nine or ten elephants were somehow in touch, just keeping their distance to avoid attracting too much attention. There was room in that kind of association-at-a-distance to still think of them as a herd, but now I felt that something was missing. It was as if Aftand had been a pivotal presence, secreting elephantine royal jelly or some other magic substance, the very smell of which held the colony together. As long as he was there, it worked. His chemical message, his assurance of cohesion even at a very diffuse level, got passed around eventually from trunk to air to mouth to Jacobson's organ and back again. Elephants as ants, but now the colony was in trouble, the network had collapsed.

There was little in 1972 to support such mystical notions, but in the next decade everything changed.

KATY PAYNE and her husband, Roger, while working on humpback whale behavior off Bermuda, discovered that the courtship song of the male was the longest and most varied sound display in the animal kingdom. Parts of it are beyond our reach, too high or too low for most human ears. Only by speeding up infrasonic or slowing down the ultrasonic components can we begin to appreciate the extraordinary complexity and sophistication of this underwater fabric of sound.

In 1984, Katy changed direction and wondered what the largest land animals did in the sound business. Just out of curiosity, she spent a week in the elephant house at the Washington Park Zoo in Oregon, recording everything that happened. While doing so, she noticed what she calls a "thrill in the air" or "silent thunder," something reminiscent not just of giant pipe organs, but also of great whales underwater. Four months later, she was back with fellow acoustic biologists from Cornell University and the equipment necessary to record and measure infrasound.

The elephant house was full of it. Later analysis showed a complex array of overlapping calls that couldn't be heard by humans in the zoo, but sprang to life and hearing when the tapes were run at ten times their usual speed. The loudest sounds were three octaves too low for us to detect, but were capable of connecting two elephants standing face to face on opposite sides of a concrete wall three feet thick.

Elephants use infrasound!

When the Cornell biologists' results were published in 1986, the world of natural history was loud with the sounds of elephant researchers kicking themselves. Of course! It was obvious in hindsight. . . .

Iain Douglas-Hamilton in Tanzania was already wondering about the ability of elephants to organize their herds without any visible or audible cues. He even joked about ESP. Cynthia Moss and Joyce Poole in Kenya were puzzled by the ability of far-flung male and female elephants to find each other during the few days in every five years when the female is available for conception. In Zimbabwe, Rowan Martin had discovered that his radio-tracked elephants were coordinating their movements with precision despite being miles apart. And flying over Botswana, I had noticed that elephant trails down to the River Chobe were not only as straight as fence lines, but parallel and equidistant, well out of sight of each other.

Silent sound solves all of these problems. At the lowest frequencies, between five and twenty-five cycles per second, infrasound has astonishing properties. The long, slow waves are hardly affected by even the densest forests and keep on going for many miles without distortion or loss of power. In the natural world, they lie somewhere just above the deep rumbles of earthquakes, volcanoes, severe weather, and ocean waves, and well below the calls of any other animals except perhaps blue and fin whales. And when Katy Payne took her equipment to Africa, even to the quietest parts of the southern and western wildernesses, she discovered that the sound of silence is everywhere punctuated, day and night, by long-distance trunk calls.

So, groups of elephants arrive at a waterhole simultaneously from different directions despite not having met for weeks. An entire herd, relaxing on its feeding grounds, suddenly takes flight or freezes in its footsteps. Groups synchronize their behavior no matter which way the wind blows. And adult males, for no apparent reason, drop whatever they are doing and converge on a female in estrus. Infrasound is the answer to all these mysteries, and the mechanism which generates many more.

The elephant network is extensive. The average animal-to-animal distance in highly populated areas may be just a few miles, but each individual is part of a far larger communication system, a cell in a network that covers hundreds of thousands of square miles, potentially an entire country. This natural internet is vast and calls into question all the assumptions we have been making about elephant society. Families can no longer be restricted to a group of visibly bonded animals. Herds could consist of every elephant in the whole ecology, which makes nonsense of all culling programs that involve taking out just family groups to prevent disturbing other groups in the area. Kill one elephant and every elephant within infrasound range knows about it instantly. Infrasound, however, also provides the kind of detail and intimacy that could help maintain hierarchies in elephant societies, like those in the Namib Desert, where individuals may not meet face to face for months or even years.

The implications of infrasound are awesome. Not least because we have now to rethink everything we have taken for granted about elephant language. It is not limited simply to the obvious and audible growls, roars, squeals, screams, and trumpets. These are, in effect, just the elephant equivalents of human shouts of encouragement or cries for help. Hidden in and below the rumbles we once attributed to indigestion there seems to be a complex, more personal vocabulary with a syntax that we are only just beginning to explore.

Just listen!

INFRASOUND is vital at Knysna. The core area of that forest covers about six hundred square miles of rugged, sometimes almost impregnable country. But with a long-wave communication system, just ten elephants could cover the area, keeping in constant touch, even if they never meet.

Their broadcasts can also be monitored. Katy Payne and her acoustic engineers at Cornell University have already begun to do just that in Ghana and the Central African Republic, eavesdropping on and documenting the calls, movement, and behavior of elusive forest elephants. They use data-analysis programs and computer mapping based on information from microphone arrays to pinpoint every animal's location. Payne's study of the rates and patterns of calling already reflects the difference between small and large groups and reveals what is going on. The next step must be computer identification of individual animals by their voiceprint, cutting human researchers in on infrasonic traffic on a bioweb elephants have been using for millions of years.

In Knysna, surveillance is far more rudimentary. It depends on ramblers walking the elephant trails or on happy accidents involving foresters and elephants who happen to coincide on the logging roads. The news from these sources is fragmentary and discouraging.

In 1980, the Forestry Department announced that despite a survey which involved two hundred workers combing the forest, only two elephants could be found—a cow and her calf—though a few days later the pair were seen in the company of an old bull. In less than ten years, it seemed, eight elephants had disappeared. Three of these were old bulls, whose deaths could have been expected because of the usual attrition that takes place when an elephant runs out of teeth. But the remaining five disappearances were mysterious, all involving elephants identified by Carter in 1970 as young or, at most, middle-aged.

In 1981, the local Wildlife Society offered a small reward for any evidence leading to the discovery of elephants, other than the three already known to exist, or the bones of dead animals. There were no takers.

In 1987, a group of hikers stumbled on two elephants—a mature cow and her teenage male offspring, presumably the same mother and child seen seven years earlier. But in 1989, the Forestry Department announced that a new calf had been born, it was assumed to the same cow and her own male offspring, though that would be highly unusual. It is more likely that an adult bull and perhaps a second cow had eluded the 1980 census—bringing the possible total back to a more encouraging, but still precarious, five elephants.

In 1990, one of the forest guards saw a cow and a year-old calf. And finally, in 1994, in response to many inquiries from the public and conservation bodies, the department left its water and forest responsibilities for the moment and mounted an intensive elephant hunt by forest workers walking two hundred yards apart through the entire core area of the usual home range. This produced the alarming conclusion that there was only *one* elephant left—a mature cow, aged about forty-five, probably the mother of the calf born in 1989!

Once again there was confusion and inexplicable disappearance. A six-year-old calf, a young bull of about twenty-five, an old bull, and perhaps a second adult cow had all vanished without trace. And the sole survivor of a herd numbering about five hundred a century before was a single female, the last Knysna elephant, known simply as the Matriarch.

ONE elephant is a conservation black joke and a biological disaster, but it has happened before. In Burundi in the 1980s. He was last seen along the course of the Rusizi River standing belly-deep in the long grass, the sole survivor of a decade-long killing spree, trunk raised in one final sad hurrah.

For the last elephant in any environment to be a female is even sadder. Cows are always part of a condominium of elephants, members of a society in which there are no individuals, just integral parts of a tight-knit feminine community, forever immersed in each other's lives and crises, sharing activities and announcements, raising each other's calves, never alone for a moment. The only sense they have of themselves is as part of something greater.

The very word "matriarch" is a compound of obligations, of an identity defined by reference to the other elephants which form her family and her clan. It is a word that has no logical or biological singular. A matriarch on her own is just an elephant, and an elephant entirely on its own is nothing.

The heartbreaking possibility of just one elephant in Knysna brought me hurrying back in the millennial year. It seemed the right thing to do. After breaking several gates, uprooting a few road signs, and bursting the tires of a logging machine at Millwood, the Matriarch seemed to have left her usual haunts. The last recorded sightings of her had been near the Big Tree, standing at the base of a microwave tower, sifting it seemed through the frequencies there, searching for any sound of other elephants.

I decided, on impulse, to look for her somewhere else, in Aftand territory on the coastal side of the new N2 national road, which now cuts off a huge chunk of the remaining indigenous forest from the rest. This, ironically, was the piece Nick Carter had recommended be fenced off as a reserve. In 1970, when traffic was slower and less severe, he had watched, enthralled, as a big bull elephant lurked in the tree cover on the mountain side of the highway, waiting until there was a lull in the traffic. Then, looking left, looking right, and then left again, he walked deliberately across the tarmac and back into the trees on the ocean side.

I could see no reason why an elephant should not, under cover of darkness, still slip across in that way. There were no fences to keep it from doing so. So I made up my mind, not just to look in the Harkerville Forest, but to approach it as I had exactly half a century before, from the seafront, from the hut, as a Strandloper should.

I HAD trouble finding the hut. There were brickworks and firebreaks and even a landing strip where springboks once grazed, plus a strange monument to the Griqua halfbreed Khoi who once rejoiced in the name of Bastards. The monument would have amused !Kamma, I thought, working my way closer to the coast, bursting out finally through the maritime forest onto a path I rembered well.

It still wound down to Sandy Bay and fisherfolk still came there in search of red roman, but the hut had vanished entirely. Recycled, I imagined, as a source of building materials for the shanty town that had sprung up outside Knysna. I wished the new owners well and the kind of uncomplicated dreams we had enjoyed on those same driftwood boards as children. Then, without a backward look, I set out westward along the clifftop path past Rooikrans and Platbank to the scree at Losklip where my older feet could even more easily slip and fall.

I didn't slip and finally came up to the rim of the gorge which had once been our boundary and was now the eastern limit of the Forest Reserve at Kranshoek. The ancient milkwood was still there, looking not a day older. What is fifty years in a life that can last a millennium?

I sat down on !Kamma's rock, the place where we first met, thinking that this would be a fine place for a memorial to him, but soon deciding that he needed none as long as one could see the distant blue-gray Outeniqua, rising steeply out of the long, slow rolls of olive hills. It was fine to be in a place where "as far as the eye can

see" means something. It is no idle boast here, but a confident state-
ment of fact. You can see almost forever. . . .

Looking inland, I saw where *fynbos* and forest had been
cleared to plant martial rows of alien pines and thought it a poor
exchange. All that was left of the patch of forest out of which we
had run in panic from a ghostly elephant was the great yellowwood that had been the focus of our attention. It was intact but,
deprived of the forest around it, showed more than a hint of nerv-
ousness, like someone caught unawares, unclothed. The sea was
just the same, rolling in almost in slow motion, leaving, even on
this fine day, a haze over the rocky coastline. I closed my eyes and
enjoyed the white noise of all this from the clifftop, letting it lap
over me, evoking other oceans, other times spent whalewatch-
ing—and when I opened my eyes, there was a whale right there!

Southern right whales are common here in the winter months,
coming in to calve in sheltered bays, but this was summer, and I
looked again. Out beyond the breakers in deep blue water a long
dark back rose gently to the surface once more and blew, or rather
blasted, a single thin column of condensation forty feet high. There
was only one whale capable of such a spout. A blue whale, the
largest animal the world has ever known! A hundred tons of sleek
grace, belying its great size, sliding slowly over until it showed just
a hint of fin before the tail flukes touched the surface. Definitely a
blue whale, one of a population gradually bouncing back from the
slaughter of the 1930s, beginning to be seen more often again.

I waited for her—female baleen whales are often larger than
their mates—to surface again, knowing from experience that she
would blow at least one more time before flicking her tail up on
the last breath before a dive, enjoying a sight that is rare from the
land. I wondered what would bring her here, so close to the coast,
during her tropical fast. Not just the scenery, surely? Then up she
came once more, another great vertical spout as she surfaced
almost horizontally, and as I watched her, I was aware of some-

thing else, of a throbbing in the air, of what Katy Payne calls "silent thunder."

IT is a sound that sneaks up on you, something you feel rather than hear, a rumble which is more visceral than cerebral, threatening to addle your mind. I rose to my feet and stared out at the whale in amazement. I knew that blue whales can make high-energy, low-frequency moans that last for thirty seconds or more, but I had never heard one before when watching blue whales off Baja California or Peru. I supposed that the sound of ship engines and generators might have masked it, but I hadn't imagined that the calls would fall within our range of hearing anyway. . . .

The sensation I was feeling on the clifftop was some sort of reverberation in the air itself. Perhaps an interference pattern set up between the whale call and its echo from the rocks below? That too seemed unlikely, and I was still puzzling over it when I realized that the whale had submerged and I was still feeling something. The strange rhythm seemed now to be coming from behind me, from the land, so I turned to look across the gorge, sweeping my gaze across the cliffs, over the great milkwood tree—and then swiftly back to the tree again, where my heart stopped.

I was twelve again, barefoot, sunburned, carefree, and riveted to the rock once again, because standing there in the shade of the tree was an elephant. A fully grown African elephant, facing left, staring out to sea! A big elephant, but this time not white or male. A female with a left tusk broken off near the base, looking for all the world like the stub of a large cigar. I had never seen this elephant before, but I knew who she was, who she had to be. I recognized her from a color photograph put out by the Department of Water Affairs and Forestry under the title "The Last Remaining

Knysna Elephant." This was the Matriarch herself. But what was she doing here?

The thunder was gone. I could no longer feel it in my bones. I was awestruck, however, both by her and by the circumstances. She hadn't been seen for months, but here she was where and when I needed her to be! That moment of hubris quickly passed as I began to understand. She was here because she no longer had anyone to talk to in the forest. She was standing here on the edge of the ocean because it was the next, nearest, and most powerful source of infrasound. The underrumble of the surf would have been well within her range, a soothing balm for an animal used to being surrounded, submerged, by low and comforting frequencies, by the lifesounds of a herd, and now this was the next-best thing!

My heart went out to her. The whole idea of this grandmother of many being alone for the first time in her life was tragic, conjuring up the vision of countless other old and lonely souls. But just as I was about to be consumed by helpless sorrow, something even more extraordinary took place. . . .

The throbbing was back in the air. I could feel it, and I began to understand why. The blue whale was on the surface again, pointed inshore, resting, her blowhole clearly visible. The Matriarch was here for the whale! The largest animal in the ocean and the largest living land animal were no more than a hundred yards apart, and I was convinced that they were communicating! In infrasound, in concert, sharing big brains and long lives, understanding the pain of high investment in a few precious offspring, aware of the importance and the pleasure of complex sociality, these rare and lovely great ladies were commiserating over the back fence of this rocky Cape shore, woman to woman, matriarch to matriarch, almost the last of their kind.

I turned, blinking away the tears, and left them to it. This was no place for a mere man. . . .

Coming
of
Age

IBU GANTI is a weaver. This is not her work, it is her life. She sits every day in the shade of a dark green breadfruit tree outside her thatched house on the hill above the village. From there she can watch all the comings and goings, and keep an eye on the fishing fleet out in the Solor Strait between her island and the other volcanic peaks which rise like sentinels out of the deep waters in this part of Indonesia.

She uses a back loom, keeping tension with her own slight body weight, leaning into a strap around her waist, passing the weft yard backward and forward in a rapid series of movements, in and out of the long lines of cotton warp. She makes ikat textiles, using threads which have already been dyed in several colors by tying them tightly at carefully calculated points in the hank. And as she weaves, a design appears magically out of the loom.

All the women in these outlying islands of Nusa Tenggara know how to weave. Some produce complex ikats in red and yellow, indigo and brown, all earth colors in wonderful traditional patterns, each intended for use in one of the important seasonal ceremonies. A very few go further, and do the impossible, turning out double ikats in which both warp and weft threads have been predyed, almost every one in a different way, in a sequence that would test the capacity of a computer. The result is a miracle, a work of great art, conjured out of the minds of women who never learned to read or write.

Ibu Ganti is one of these, perhaps the best of them, because her designs are unique and ever-changing. Most of the weavers produce old well-worn patterns that are typical of the island, birds and flowers, spirits and houses, and sometimes manta rays, this last to be worn only at the ritual dedication of outrigger boats setting out for the annual hunt of passing sperm whales. But Ibu Ganti is different. Her father was a charcoal-maker, and Ganti weaves what only Ganti sees and nobody else understands.

Her ikats are exquisite, woven tightly and well, each one the work of a year or more. And every piece glows with the vibrant procession through it of herds of elephants, tusked and tuskless, bulls, cows, and calves, fresh from their immersion in a forest pool, making their way down the slopes to feed on palm fruit in the grasslands, relishing one another in the way elephants will. These are not just formal patterns, symbolic elephants, based on hearsay or some antique convention. These are fresh portraits, taken directly from life, which is very strange, because Ibu Ganti has never left the island, and the nearest elephant is a species that once lived on old Celebes, six hundred miles away, and has been extinct there since the last Ice Age!

CHAPTER SEVEN

Imagining the Elephant

> Formerly, elephants could go anywhere they
> pleased and assume any shape; they roamed as
> they liked in the sky and on the earth.
> —MATANGA-LILA of Nilakantha, tenth century

SOMETHING strange is going on.

Something obvious, it seems, only to those young enough, tipsy enough, or creative enough to notice. I can't believe, however, that this revelation is necessarily confined to the innocent, the inebriate, and the inspired. That is a fine sample of our species, but there must be more to it. After meeting Lukie, Malachy, and Ibu Ganti, I wondered what else they might have in common—apart from elusive elephants.

All three lived in the country, away from the distractions of urban life, but not in elephant country, though none of them considered their experience unusual. On the contrary, each was surprised that everybody wasn't seeing what they saw, and impatient with those who doubted. And all were reserved, shy, and, perhaps because of their experiences, slow to draw attention to themselves.

I only got to hear about Lukie because I work with his father, Malachy because I live not far away, and Ibu Ganti because I happened to see a sample of her work. So I was perhaps the most obvious common factor. There seemed to be no other similarities, but there was one important difference. They all saw elephants, but not the *same* elephants.

Ibu Ganti was the easiest to assess, because she had produced vivid images of her experience. Her woven elephants were elegant, with gently curving tusks, triangular ears, long tails, humped backs, and small heads with high, double domes. They were unquestionably Asian elephants, but differed just enough from the usual Indian form to raise suspicions they were not *Elephas maximus*, but perhaps the extinct island form known from fossils found on Sulawesi and identified as *Elephas celebensis*.

Malachy was also persuasive. He described an elephant with a shaggy coat, hugely curved tusks, tiny ears, a short tail, a deeply sloped back, and a very high domed head "with a brush cut." A very good likeness to the woolly mammoth *Mammuthus primigenius*, which has been found frozen and was very common in the colder parts of Europe, until it too disappeared under the double threat of human hunting and the Ice Age.

But it was Lukie who offered the most interesting detail. He couldn't describe his elephants directly, but responded with total certainty when he was shown pictures of living elephants and several extinct species known to have existed in North America. He had no hesitation in picking out the mastodon *Mammut americanum*, which we believe had curved tusks, small ears, a straight back, and an undistinguished low brow. And appropriately, it is also a species well known from early Pleistocene deposits in Florida. A complete mastodon was only recently recovered from Silver River just a few miles away.

Each of the three people had unusual access to information about, and apparently direct experience of, the kind of elephant that once lived in or near their homes. Every one of those elephants ought to have vanished with the last glaciation, along with woolly rhinos, cave bears, giant ground sloths, and saber-toothed cats, but not one of the three individuals mentioned any of the other impressive megafauna.

So why just elephants?

Could it be because they may still be around? There could, for instance, be pockets of surviving mammoths in sparsely populated areas of Siberia. But in Ireland? Doubtful. I believe there is an even more intriguing possibility. One that goes back to my discussions with Raymond Dart about Jacobson's organ, and with Alister Hardy about the paranormal.

Mammals are "supersmellers." We have the best noses in the business. Our nasal chambers are so vast that they compete with the brain for space in our skulls. And at the front of our faces, the nose opens to the outside air in a wonderful array of structures that range all the way from the flat muscular nostril valve in whales to the extended and expressive proboscis of elephants.

Mammals are also scent factories. Our warm blood brews up an aromatic chemistry against which even flowers cannot compete. And the odors seep out into the world through every possible aperture in our soft skins, scattering very personal information about like aromatic confetti. We each have a unique olfactory signature, and as part of this is genetic and duplicated in our closest relatives, we also come to smell "familiar," sharing a hive or colony identity that we find reassuring.

Smell is not a secret system. The air is full of messages, often conflicting ones, so signals can get crossed. Female pigs, for instance, are persuaded to dig up truffles because these cunning fungi produce steroids identical to those on the breath of a lusty boar. The sow is disappointed, but the truffle spores get distributed anyway. The "odornet" needs to be public to be useful, so despite such confusion, the lines stay open.

One way of minimizing crossed lines is to make messages sex-specific. In humans, musk is a male hormone, one that goes undetected by half of the world's men, usually the ones who wear too much cologne. Women, on the other hand, are able to detect musk even at dilutions as low as one part in a million. And their sensitivity to this, and all male hormones, reaches its peak precisely at the moment of ovulation. A system that has served our species well.

Another way of making sure that a fragrant note gets to its proper destination is to package it in ways that are accessible not to ordinary smell, but to the more restricted sensitivity of the rival system involving Jacobson's organ.

The primary role of mainline smell seems to be analyzing odors which have no predetermined meaning. The organ of Jacobson, however, specializes in instinctive recognition of odors that carry specific information about gender and reproductive and dominance status. And the organ passes this news on, not to the forebrain, but to the old limbic system at the back of the brain, where all such basic matters are still organized—and perhaps stored away in long-term memory.

At Warwick University in England, John Kinge is concerned with the elusive connection between smell and memory and uses a "nostalgia pack" of trigger odors designed to evoke memories of the early 1940s. He uses pads soaked in scents identified simply as Old Teapot or Air Raid Shelter to conjure up long-forgotten memories in old soldiers now suffering from Alzheimer's syndrome. The effect is dramatic. One almost comatose veteran found to his astonishment that after just one sniff of the disinfectant in Field Hospital, he was able to rattle off his wartime rifle number.

The interesting thing about all fragrances is that they tend to be experiences of the moment, with none of the usual texture of time and space. Being freeform, they are very difficult to encode and file away in the places where most other memories go. Important smells, the ones that change our lives, seem to get imprinted somewhere deep in the brain in a form that gives them extraordinary clarity. So such odor-linked memories tend to come back to us with all their flavors intact, even after many years.

Smell is an emotional sense rather than an intellectual one. It is more right-brain than left-brain, more intuitive than logical, and therefore more likely to be unconsciously than consciously perceived. All of which appears to make odor-linked memories almost impossible to forget. They come to us, more often than not, via Jacobson's organ and constitute a vital primitive protection system, making it possible for us to learn, often in one short trial, that something is dangerous and needs to be avoided in future. So long-term odor memory is a highly adaptive system, with huge evolutionary significance. Something that acts as the body's advance guard, giving us instant access to significant past events with the kind of clarity no other memory system can match.

And that saves lives. . . .

THERE is a record of a bloodhound in Bennington, Vermont, which succeeded in picking up a scent trail that was eight days old. It followed this into a grocery store and a bank, sniffing the ground and higher up on bushes and buildings, crossing several busy streets until it ended at a bench outside the local bus station. The missing man later confirmed he had followed that precise route before sitting there as he waited to board a bus to California.

Bloodhounds find us naked apes easy prey. Every day we shed forty million flakes of skin, each one supporting a rich flora of bacteria with characteristic odors. All this invisible and odorous dandruff drifts along behind us in a vapor trail, leaving a track that can leap out at a hound more than a week later. Even on a quiet day, we produce several pints of sweat, the smell of which is so distinctive that most dogs can retrieve a pebble from a riverbed and return it to the hand of the man who threw it. In one laboratory test, a beagle identified the single glass slide in a box that had been touched briefly by one human fingertip six weeks previously.

Bloodhounds and beagles have about 300 million olfactory sense cells in their noses, arranged into a tissue whose total area would cover something about the size of this page. It is thought that a single human skin cell landing on this sensitive surface could be all a hound needs to keep it after its quarry. Compared to us, with just six million smell cells, they may be a million times more sensitive to social odors, but we also have a secret weapon. . . .

We seldom, if ever, experience any sensation in isolation. Our senses feed on one another, shuffling, sorting, reinforcing, blending as they go, and, strangely, nothing is lost in the mix. The separate senses are not so much diluted as reinvigorated, giving some blind people the chance to "see" as well as any sighted person. This will not be news to many poets, artists, and musicians who routinely inhabit synesthetic worlds. Shelley celebrated "music so soft it felt like an odor," and Rimsky-Korsakov insisted that the key of E major was "bright blue."

Our noses mix and match most of the time, taking up information in any way they can, combining news, both volatile and odorless, in ways that give us powers still hard to describe. I think that in this synesthetic harmony may lie the secrets of knowing things apparently unknowable, and recalling things with the sort of emotional clarity and immediacy that appears to be unavailable to everyday memory.

IT is possible to know things we should not know, and to see things we could not possibly see. In fact, what we call intuition may be no more than an idea which rises, without bidding, to conscious attention as a result of an unconscious stimulus. Something perhaps as small as a single cell falling on our sparse olfactory receptors, but magnified there by another sense, or by the action of a brain far larger than any bloodhound's. We make up in gray matter what we lack in olfactory acuity, allowing some of us, handicapped perhaps by loss of sight or hearing, to recognize the smell of another person well out of sight and beyond normal hearing.

I wonder what happens to all those forty million cells, something like a soup plate full, that we lose every day? They slough off all the time, ten thousand cells an hour from every fingertip, creating a cloud in our wake. Some must be short-lived, shriveling up and blowing away like dust. Others probably last longer, lingering in bedsheets, carpets, and clothes, protected from destruction for a while. But there must be a few persistent ones which, if they can avoid being consumed by mites, could live on for years. In the right circumstances maybe even for centuries. Who knows what our noses may make of those?

The essential message may still be intact, even in a single discarded cell preserved in a tomb or a hollow tree. But the chances are that any information it once carried will be diluted and fragmentary, rather low on characterization, reduced from a fully fleshed-out autobiography to something more like a classified ad. But even that could still be useful to a bloodhound or a human with a good nose. There may be just enough surviving information, the bare minimum necessary to trigger some sort of synesthetic effect, enough to dress up an illusion, perhaps even in appropriate period costume, as a complete "ghost"!

I have tried for years to make sense of ghosts. Most are sedentary, fixed to a particular location as if something of them still survives there. Most are clothed, which, as Alister Hardy pointed out, is hard to explain, even if you can accept the possibility of spirit survival. But spirit socks and frocks? I am encouraged, however, to learn that some ghosts do have a characteristic smell. That may be a use-ful clue. Smell, in the end, may be our last resort, all that connects us to the provider of the stimulus, the previous owner of the cells.

Smell is certainly a potent channel of communication, but its vocabulary is rather limited and sometimes provides us with only a hazy outline, a very sketchy biography, something of limited intelli-gence—which is actually a very good description of most spirits I have encountered. They tend to be high on emotional impact, all those moans and groans, but very low on useful facts about the great beyond. They are, in fact, more or less exactly what you would expect from a single molecular message or a brief smellogram.

But if the cells were once attached to someone you knew per-sonally, the result could be very different. You could find yourself confronted, not just by a vague impression, but by a full synesthetic symphony of all the senses, including words and pictures, tastes and textures, everything necessary for a complex and completely con-vincing illusion!

ALL of which brings me back to elephants, and in particular to the mysterious white elephant.

Once I knew that Lukie, Malachy, and Ibu Ganti were experi-encing something with local relevance, with elephants appropriate to their place, if not their time, I began to think seriously about my own experiences. Kroos Arend and I appear to have been confronted by the same phenomenon. We were party to the same illusion, perhaps. That of a large elephant, more like an African than an Asian form, smooth-skinned rather than hairy, with a big head and very long, straight tusks. More like a Knysna elephant than an Addo one, not a typical forest animal, but unlike either in one important respect. It appeared and disappeared without warning, and looked light-colored, paler than an elephant ought to be. Perhaps because its reality was less than complete, maybe even a little "ghostly"?

That made some kind of sense. I have often wondered why ghosts should be so washed-out. We never hear of technicolor hauntings involving vivid costumes, bright eyes, and scarlet lipsticks. Visitations tend to be faded and sallow, the kind of thing most often impersonated by an idiot in a white sheet. Which is not surprising if they come to us by courtesy of a feeble tissue, ekeing out its dim existence in some convenient cranny.

I tried to produce my own sketch of the white bull, a sort of proboscid Identikit. And as I did this, and came up with something that bore a passing resemblance to my memory, it began to ring other bells for me. It began to look familiar, not from the Knysna forest, but from reconstructions of extinct elephants!

It began to take on a distinct likeness to several elephants depicted from the Plio-Pleistocene of southern Africa, going back perhaps as far as twelve million years. The problem with most such studies is that classification depends on the nature of the grinding teeth, which neither Kroos nor I had ever seen. We had concentrated on the tusks, but these too tended to be wildly different in each reconstruction, based on little more than a best guess. The animal that bore the closest resemblance to our phantom was one with long straight tusks, found on the Cape Coast about five million years ago and identified as one of the ancestral gomphotheres—the beasts that were bolted together. This one, once widespread in Africa, belonged to the genus *Anancus* and apparently had tusks long enough to trip over.

My experience of the white bull had been confined to the clifftop near Losklip, which, at that time, was untouched *fynbos* backed by virgin forest. I had seen him first in the shade of an ancient milkwood tree above the sea. In a place which would have been special even without a ghostly elephant. It was rich in the kinds of energies that make a spot attractive to other animals, whose predilection inspires humans looking for a spiritual site on which to settle. Wherever holy places exist, they are accompanied by legends that tell of their discovery. They are revealed as a result of some divine omen, or they are found because someone had a vision or a dream about them. And if no account is given, then you can be certain that the new shrine was built on top of an old one, that the chosen site was already one of traditional sanctity, and that the tale of its original revelation will be one of this kind.

The choice of such places for settlement or worship is always the result of inspiration rather than intellection. It just feels right and good. In any other part of the world, this clifftop would have a shrine or a monastery upon it. It already does in my imagination, but even before I arrived, it was different from any other site on the same coastline. This was where I was inspired and came into the presence, not only of a phantom elephant, but of an extraordinary man. Who came first, the elephant or !Kamma? It is still not very clear to me. . . .

KROOS AREND'S encounters with the white bull and !Kamma occurred further inland, near a giant yellowwood in what is now known as the Garden of Eden.

It is interesting how names, the good ones, so often reflect the character of a place, keeping its magic alive. Once again, it is hard to decide which came first, the site or the spell. But I suspect that this popular picnic spot was once connected to mystery by the *houtkappers*, whose forest lore also gave Phantom Pass its menacing reputation. And who knows how much of woodcutter consciousness was influenced, in its turn, by contact with the original forest people, the Outeniqua Khoi?

However it started, Kroos first met his white elephant as a child, a thoughtful young man with something else on his mind. Someone in a state of detachment, the sort of mind-set most conducive to meditation and transcendence. A mind perfectly prepared for dealing with subtle sensations, perhaps even ones as vanishingly small as a single cell bearing subliminal information?

I am scrambling here, trying to make sense of something that may not be amenable to this kind of interpretation at all, but I am encouraged by what we do know about elephants' skins.

Despite the name "pachyderm," which means "thick skin," an elephant's hide is not particularly thick, not for an animal of its size. On the back and sides, it may be more than an inch deep, but nowhere is it leathery and insensitive. Mosquitoes and biting flies easily draw blood and irritate the sparse hairs that concentrate around eyes, ears, chin, and tail, making elephants distinctly ticklish. A whole ecology of external hitchhikers and parasites colonize the many deep wrinkles and creases on its head and belly. And the heavy folds of its baggy pants are deep enough to provide cover for a nest of enterprising rats. Given this vast and delicate pasture, it is no surprise that all elephants love bathing and quicken their steps as they near a favorite pool. Wallowing, splashing, and playing there, no matter how young or old, they take every advantage of water to dislodge parasites or bake them in a dry mud crust that can be knocked off later against a convenient tree or rock. Flapping, wrestling, scratching each other with their tusks, or with a stick or palm frond held in the trunk and used as a flyswatter, elephants are constantly scraping away, losing wheelbarrow loads of dry skin flakes, some small enough to blow away, carrying with them all the olfactory and genetic information necessary to identify, and perhaps even clone, a new individual.

There are more than enough of such traces left blowing in the wind, caught in crevices, or entombed in mud packs under circumstances that could fossilize them, erode them, and recycle them millions of years later. Africa, in particular, must be liberally dusted with molecules of "elephantness," ready available for later sampling. The surprise is that more of it doesn't get around and work its strange magic on more people, not in the form of "pink elephants," but more or less real white ones made pale by the nature of their manifestation.

Perhaps it does. Something similar seems to be happening in Britain. . . .

FOR many years now, there have been sporadic sightings of big black cats in the countryside. It began in 1976 with one so large it became known as the Beast of Bodmin Moor and was identified by several naturalists as a black panther, the melanistic form of the American cougar or mountain lion. What it was doing loose in Cornwall is another matter.

George Ridpath, a police officer in Scotland, has spent twenty-five years following up such feline reports in the County of Fife. He has plaster casts and photographs of paw prints and kills of deer and sheep that look remarkably like the work of a leopard. He believes there may be more than one, perhaps as many as three, all black, operating in the lowlands.

Photographs of these big cats are rare and, on the whole, unconvincing. There is so much about the accounts that is frag-mentary, and hard evidence is so difficult to come by, that most sci-entists haven't taken the stories very seriously. After the flurry of reports in the 1970s, things quieted down for a while, but in 2000 there were five sightings in a single month. The most extraordinary was an attack on an eleven-year-old boy near Monmouth in the Welsh hills. Josh Hopkins was left with three unquestionable claw marks from what he described as a great black cat the size of a labrador. The depth and spacing of the wounds on his left cheek are consistent with panther claw marks.

In 1976, the British government passed the Dangerous Wild

Animals Act, prohibiting private citizens from keeping large predators as pets, and it is possible that the first rush of stories could have
involved animals simply released instead of destroyed at that time.
But most big cats don't live much more than twenty years, so the
implication of the recent outbreak is not only that large cats are still
living wild in Britain, but that they are breeding.

If that were not enough to give mothers sleepless nights, there
also appear to be mysterious big black dogs at large, not just in
Britain, but also in France, Ireland, Italy, and Croatia. These have
been growling in the European dark for centuries and even carry
local names such as Shag, Padfoot, and Barghest. They are associated with burial grounds, footpaths, and the sites of old gallows, and
are often seen at times of violent crimes. Their eyes, of course, glow
red in the dark and many of them slaver at the mouth. But the most
striking and suggestive feature of these scary creatures is that they
are often seen to walk through solid objects and melt away.

There is clearly a traditional, almost mythic, quality to the dogs.
They are way out of the ordinary, drawing more on folklore and
supersition than they do on natural history. But the cats, apart from
their color, are more solid. They have drawn blood on at least one
occasion and may be more amenable to objective investigation.

To me, they feel rather like my white elephant, the product both
of nature and the imagination.

I BELIEVE, along with British biologist Nicholas Humphrey, that
we are involved in everything that happens. Each one of us takes
part in what he calls "weaving the illusion of reality," and only
artists have the vision to unravel such conceits and show us what
truly lies within. Picasso defined his art as "the lie that helps us to
see the truth."

But even that isn't enough. Only part of what is perceived comes through the senses anyway, the remainder comes from within, and it is very difficult to decide which is which. I don't know what to believe, or what to make of my experiences at Knysna. They seem so far-fetched in the telling, but as Dart often said, "I have a sneaking feeling" that there is something here worth pursuing. Something that might help understand "haunting" in general. Perhaps even account for the persistent feeling among those recently bereaved, and still living with familiar belongings and fragrances, that those who have died are not far gone. I know dozens who, sometimes in half-light or half awake, have experienced very detailed and convincing visions of the dead.

Extinct elephants are harder to account for, but I also suspect that the Knysna situation is an unusual one. I continue to be drawn to it, partly by my own experiences there, but partly because it seems so concentrated. A vanishingly small herd in a constantly diminishing habitat, hanging on against all the odds, provides a finer focus than can be brought to bear in Amboseli or the forests of the Central African Republic. And I suggest that this distillation of flesh and space not only keeps me engrossed, but may have a similar collective influence on the surviving elephants. Nothing concentrates the mind better than an impending death sentence.

It seems very clear to me that the Addo and the Knysna elephants I have known are not ordinary elephants. They are different as a direct consequence of their proximity to people in growing numbers, with more and more intrusive machinery. They have had to change their behavior, and they have done so in a very creative fashion.

The classical picture of elephant evolution involves a number of specific changes. Since the beginning of the Oligocene, perhaps forty million years ago, successful proboscids have been the ones that have increased in size and weight; lengthened their leg bones and broadened their feet to support this great mass; grown larger skulls, but kept these reasonably light with many air spaces; shortened the neck to support such a large head; specialized the molar teeth as efficient grinders of rough food; allowed their incisors to grow into impressive tusks; and developed a unique multipurpose trunk.

Dress all these modifications and adaptations up together in a baggy suit and you have a typical modern elephant like the African savanna form *Loxodonta africanus*.

Such a simple sequence makes it look easy, but there were many false starts and dead ends, mutations that went nowhere. We know of hundreds of failed experiments, extinct species thrown up and thrown out by the beginning of the Miocene, some fifteen million years later. The sheer abundance of hopeful fossils in the proboscidean tree is proof at least of evolutionary vigor, of a trend that seemed to offer enough success at each stage of development to keep the program running. Five million years ago, at the end of the Miocene, there were dozens of species, representing five main lines of development, occupying every continent but Australia and Antarctica. Today there are only two lines, one in Asia, represented by a single species, the other in Africa, with prehaps two species, all surviving because they have become key species, maintaining biodiversity and shaping environments in their own areas. But all are also threatened by a direct challenge from another widespread, tool-using, earth-moving, and earth-shaking species—*Homo sapiens*.

The prognosis is not good. Fragmented habitats, large-scale agricultural developments, and rampant population growth now threaten the survival of proboscids everywhere. The least optimistic estimates warn of the demise of all wild elephants in a couple of our generations. There are a number of human programs dedicated to fighting for of elephants, but perhaps the best news of all is that elephants themselves are beginning to fight back. . . .

MUSTH in domestic Asian elephants has been well known for centuries, mainly because it makes males aggressive and upsets work
schedules. People there learned long ago to give such males a wide
berth. Until twenty years ago, the scientific consensus was that
musth did not occur at all in Africa. But in 1981, Joyce Poole and
Cynthia Moss published a study which made it clear that all African
elephants by the age of twenty-five do come into musth at a specific
time of the year, and this always leads to heightened sexual and
aggressive behavior.

Poole, more recently, explored the role of such aggression.
Game theory—a mathematical measure of gain and loss in competitive situations—predicts that in warfare or animal behavior, it is
counterproductive to let your opponent know exactly what you
intend to do. "I am going to attack you" is a useful signal only if it
is irrevocable, because no behavioral act exists in isolation. It is
part of a long series of such acts in which you have to be consistent
and follow through. Bluffers and cheaters don't benefit in the long run.

But elephants, it turns out, are a lot more subtle. All bulls keep
up to date on the reproductive state of all other bulls in the area and
reassess their role in every possible conflict by making allowances
for other males in musth. Those individuals who are in musth have
a reproductive advantage—they are more likely to be accepted by
estrous females—and that possibility is factored into any decision on
whether to attack or not. If your opponent is in musth and you are
not, there is no point in fighting him even if you are bigger and
stronger. So you retract your honest announcement of aggression
and back off. But if both of you are in musth, then the smaller,
younger male will retract, not just by physically giving way, but by
deliberately turning off the hormonal tap that makes him so aggres-

sive. So much for game theory and its founder, John von Neumann; elephants know better.

Those working with elephants in the wild have to learn to read them in the same subtle way, recognizing individuals, recording their musth cycles, noticing how recently any male has encountered an unguarded estrous female or was himself attacked by a higher-ranking musth male, looking for the telltale dark areas near the temporal gland which warn that this animal means business, his taps are open, whatever his other signals may seem to be saying. . . .

So far so good, but more and more often these days, elephants are not totally wild. They are fenced "as wild"; or they are semiwild and being fed some of the time; or they are semicaptive, becoming very used to having people around; or they are fully domesticated, kept under some kind of control all the time. And the situation in all of the last three categories is complicated by the fact that many of the elephants involved are "salvaged," rescued when young from a cull (let's be honest about it, they are the survivors of a messy massacre) of all the adults in their herd.

These elephants are always going to be unpredictable, partly because of lasting trauma, but mostly because they miss out on the chance to learn how to behave as elephants. They are deprived of all the niceties and subtleties that can only be learned from adult animals. And it is becoming abundantly clear that young elephants from broken herds are as wayward and rootless and socially inept as human children from broken homes.

It all began in South Africa in the early 1980s, when the Kruger National Park decided to deal with its growing population of elephants by a controversial culling program. The technique involved darting adult animals from the air and then shooting them from the ground, in the presence of the youngsters, who were rounded up and exported to other parks and reserves where elephants have long since disappeared.

"The young elephants are hunted, captured, transported, and shunted into smaller, closed reserves," said one anonymous ecologist. "And not nearly enough research has been done on such practices. We are beginning to see warning signs that, in the best interests of conservation, we have been playing God to elephants without thought for the consequences."

THE problem became crucial about fifteen years later as the cute little orphans reached their late teens and early twenties and began to produce testosterone.

In 1993, a group of foreign tourists in an open-air vehicle at Hluhluwe Game Reserve came close to death after being repeatedly charged by a bull elephant. In 1995, a German tourist was trampled to death in the showpiece Pilanesberg Game Reserve near the resort of Sun City. In 1996, a young "rogue" bull attacked another group in the same reserve, and on the following day killed the professional hunter sent out to shoot him.

Humans are not the only targets. Gangs of antisocial young male elephants in several parks around South Africa have begun to show increasing signs of pathological behavior. At Pilanesberg, they attacked, tried to rape, and gored to death nineteen rare and valuable white rhinos.

Such meaningless, motiveless, uncontrolled aggression is not normal. It does not occur in undisturbed elephant populations. At least part of the problem appears to be early trauma, stress, and translocation, but the main factor is almost certainly the lack of adult discipline in their lives.

Matriarchs and other adult female elephants play an enormous role in socializing young elephants. Elephants learn by example, by direct instruction from mothers who may even lead a daughter to the "right" male and guide her through the etiquette of courtship. And in most herds, it is clear that teenage elephants do not make the best mothers. Grandmothers often have to help out.

Apart from matriarchal discipline, young bulls also need adult male instruction. Mature bulls in or near the herd are a stabilizing presence. They provide balance, especially at the difficult time when teenage males are coming into musth for the first time, having to deal with their own unfocused aggressive tendencies. Then the presence of older, more mature bulls is vital. Competition with them forces younger, smaller, less experienced males to retract and calm down. Without this kind of restraint, the young bulls are far more likely to take their frustration out on other individuals, even those of other species.

Pilanesberg learned the lesson and began to introduce adult male elephants into the hierarchy at the reserve, hoping to rearrange the society and deal with the adolescent delinquents. The researcher involved in this program was Andre Klocke, a leading South African expert on elephant behavior, who later went on to Botswana to work for Elephant Back Safaris at Abu Camp.

This is a concession on the edge of the Okavango, where small groups of tourists are introduced to the glories of the swamp, riding on the backs of elephants that carry them past lions and through lily-clad lagoons. It is a superb way of getting close to wildlife and going where no other vehicle could pass without damaging the environment. It is ecotourism at its best, but it involves a definite risk.

Abu is a forty-year-old elephant, a senior partner in the enterprise, rescued and returned from a small American zoo. Cathy, the mature matriarch, is another returnee who once starred opposite Clint Eastwood in *White Hunter, Black Heart*. Together they provide a stable presence, but the rest of the safari herd are "cull orphans" with checkered histories.

Klocke and his colleagues have been involved in the Botswana Elephant Training and Film School, the first such venture in southern Africa, designed to train adolescent elephants and new mahouts.

They use gentle verbal commands to control their charges, doing everything they can to integrate the young recruits into a functional elephant herd, but there are inevitable wild cards in this game.

On May 4, 2000, Klocke and his team were unsaddling the elephants at the end of a routine safari when, without warning, a twenty-eight-year-old bull turned on him, drove its tusks into his body, and threw him high into the air. Klocke, the same age as Nyaka Nyaka, died instantly. And on the following day, the elephant too was destroyed. Both dying as a result of misunderstanding.

Like Klocke, Nyaka Nyaka had come to the camp from Pilanesberg, where he had earned the reputation of being a "problem elephant." Nothing is known about his early history except that he was captured as a calf in Namibia, but the chances are that his experience of people was both negative and limited. At Abu Camp, he went through a period of difficult adjustment to captivity, but he seemed to settle well, and that, ironically, may have been the direct cause of the tragedy. It was not an accident.

Nyaka Nyaka was well into his majority and would certainly have begun his musth cycle. Andre Klocke was an integral part of the herd hierarchy at the camp, a high-ranking male, but unfortunately incapable of taking part in the subtle hormonal exchanges that govern the relationship of bull elephants. As an expert in elephant behavior, Klocke would have noticed and known this elephant's sexual condition. But as a rival male, he was ill-equipped to signal: "No contest. I'm not in musth. You don't have to worry about me!"

A reporter, covering the event for a South African newspaper, asked the spokesperson for the safari company if the elephants were unpredictable. She answered firmly: "No. We know elephants and we work with them all the time. None of us can understand why Nyaka Nyaka should have attacked Andre!"

Precisely. It was a family affair. That's where most homicides occur.

THE Knysna elephants are not in captivity. They are the only truly wild, free-range, unfenced elephants left in South Africa. But they are severely restricted. Their present forest range would not, under normal conditions, be a permanent habitat. They once lived also in the foothills of the Outeniquas, on open grasslands, and in marshy wetlands, but have been forced to retreat by farmers, miners, and urban development.

Nevertheless, they have shown an amazing ability to adapt to human interference and human presence, even in the last stronghold of the indigenous forest. They have become, even in the restricted human sense of the word, highly "sophisticated."

Nick Carter, in 1970, noted that Knysna was a relatively busy forest. "Only in the deepest, darkest *kloofs* is there complete silence. Distant power saws and crashing lorries can often be heard from afar, when least expected." And yet, he observed, the elephants did not seem to worry unduly. "They moved a short way if they had to, and then, as often as not, moved back again. Was it possible that these animals were getting so accustomed to human activity that they could sum it up and distinguish real danger from ordinary disturbance?"

Absolutely. My brief exposure to the Knysna herd confirms that. The logging operations in the forest are far more extensive now, based mainly on commercial plantings of pines and eucalypts that have replaced a good percentage of the indigenous forest even in my lifetime. There are more roads, bigger trucks, heavier machinery, greater tourist traffic, including helicopters—altogether a more industrial approach to the forest than before. And yet the elephants manage to go their own way so successfully that most local people have never seen one.

I believe that sightings are so rare simply because the elephants have changed, both physically and psychologically.

Elephants in the Addo responded to their circumstances by becoming smaller, tuskless, more compact, more cautious, and, when necessary, more aggressive. All changes that reflect their ancestral origins as forest elephants. This is described by geneticists as "regression," but it is entirely appropriate to the problems facing them in the succulent bushland. From what I have seen and heard, the Knysna elephants have moved in another direction. They remain robust, well-tusked, well-fed, savanna-style elephants. Aggressive when pushed, but cautious in a far more calculated way.

You can see it in their eyes. . . .

EVERY book, every study of elephants everywhere, makes a point about their eyesight. They say it is notoriously bad, generally poor, at best no more than moderate.

Some make much of the fact that completely blind elephants seem to manage perfectly well. Others point out that elephants are largely nocturnal, have tiny eyes, and seem not to see things well, even in daylight, until they move. The truth is that elephant's eyes are far larger than ours, almost two inches in diameter, with an iris that is usually hazel in color and a round pupil. In the open, in bright sunlight, they do, very sensibly, tend to travel with eyes half hooded. But in the shade, in the shelter of the forest, they take on a very different aspect.

The eyelids are nearly always open wide, wrinkling about the socket in a way that suggests concentration. The pupils zoom in and out in direct relation to the emotional value of what is being seen. And the long, straggling eyelashes flutter, dark against the creamy cornea.

Everything about the eye at close quarters is alluring. Well, that was the way I felt about Delilah. And she could see me coming from halfway across the zoo.

The distance between an elephant's eyes is huge. They lie right on the edge of the orbit, so even though an elephant has little ability to turn its head, it has unexpectedly good rear-view vision, very useful for reversing. Which elephants often do. To see forward, and get any kind of binocular vision, an elephant must raise its head and look down its nose, which can be very off-putting because it brings the tusks up into the fixed-bayonet position. Which is the way one most often sees a Knysna elephant—*en garde!*

Bruce Kinloch and Nick Carter had the same impression about the size of the eyes in Knysna elephants. They seem to be larger than normal, and always watchful. Carter concluded: "Their eyesight is certainly much keener than any other elephant I have ever encountered and has on several occasions proved most disconcerting." He was spotted one day by an upwind cow at a distance of about two hundred yards. "It may be possible," he said, "that their long sojourn in the forest gloom has sharpened their eyesight to an interesting degree."

Workers on forest elephants in the Central African Republic comment in the same vein about the vision of their charges. It does seem that in low light at least, elephant eyesight is actually quite good. They have all the necessary retinal and optical equipment, and it would not require a new genetic mutation to acquire better vision. Merely the unmasking of an old forest adaptation. One more example of a selection pressure applied by humans, and responded to with alacrity—in about twenty elephant generations—by a species in the febrile environment of the Cape Coast.

Almost everyone I know who has ever seen a Knysna elephant says much the same thing: "In the open, the most expressive part of an elephant is its trunk. In the forest, it is the eyes you notice. Sometimes it is all you see, peering through the foliage. And always they look right at you, not blankly, but with deliberation and obvious intelligence. You can almost see them thinking!"

IT is difficult, probably impossible, to rank the relative value of the senses in any other species. There is little enough agreement about our own.

Aristotle put sight at the top, and followed it with each of the other senses according to their vertical position on the human body. Diogenes gave pride of place to forthright smell, and Hippocrates to the beauties of sound and the ability to hear music. But for all people, and presumably all other mammals, who live in forest where vision is limited, smell becomes the most definitive sense. There is little or no wind under the canopy, and odor lingers so long that you can invariably smell farther than you can see. There is always a baseline, a musty background scent of decaying vegetation, but anything over and above that becomes very conspicuous, like a bright light on a dark night, providing useful information.

Elephants use smell all the time. They "hoover" the environment, sifting through all its news at regular intervals, matching it with olfactory memories of every place they know, searching for the inconsistencies that mean something has changed, and isolating the bits that need immediate attention. And in all this, they are served by two elephantine advantages—a big brain and the largest Jacobson's organ in the business.

Size, of course, isn't everything. Memory is closer to the truth. We are born with a tendency to respond to the smell of our mothers, but very little else is fixed. Most of the rest we have to learn, largely by trial and error and by social example. We acquire our odor memory from experience. Where we keep it remains mysterious, but electrical mapping of the brain suggests that smell touches us in both cerebral hemispheres, exciting emotional activity on the right side at first, leading later to intellectual activity—such as trying to remember the name of a particular perfume—on the left. Similar studies on elephants show that a major part of the brain, perhaps as much as two-thirds, is directly involved with olfactory information. And a good part of the rest is stimulated by the effect of hormonal cues received via the largest Jacobson's organ in the world.

Our memory of important odors is simple, direct, and largely unconscious, very resistant to decay or later interference. This is what makes long-term memories so hard to articulate. They have a "tip-of-the-nose" quality. We recognize them, but find them very hard to label or identify in words. They go directly into the limbic system, and if the same is true of the elephant, this would help to make sense of the old adage that elephants never forget.

It could be true. A pioneering experiment in Germany on acoustic discrimination by Asian elephants showed that not only did they have perfect pitch, but they could recall and respond to complex pairs of tones as much as a year later. Their memory for visual patterns was almost as acute.

One of the best measurements of brain efficiency or relative intelligence is the weight ratio between the reptilian old brain and the new mammalian cortex. This provides values of 1:14 for pigs, 1:48 for baboons, and 1:170 for humans. Elephants fit into this spectrum at 1:104, midway between our fellow primate and ourselves. This is, however, an index which undervalues what we now know still happens in the old brain of elephants and ourselves. If allowance is made for the major role the brainstem and Jacobson's organ play in olfactory sensitivity and memory, we and the elephants are neck and neck, nose to nose.

There is abundant evidence to confirm that elephants do have a good long-term memory. So what if part of this is very long indeed, going all the way back to *Anancus*? Do elephants have the kind of recall that might lead to visions of their ancestors? Does my experience of the white phantom depend on the continued existence of the present Knysna herd? Do we all enjoy elephants because they touch us in this way and make us think?

Is this how it all works? Have I been seeing things?

PSYCHIATRY defines "hallucination" as "apparent perception of an external object when no such object is present" and usually diagnoses it as a result of seizures, sleep deprivation, drug reactions, substance abuse, grief, stress, disease, or a whole host of neurological insults. But what if it is not an insult, but a blessing? Not a disorder, but a normal and useful part of perception? It may be relatively uncommon, and in some quarters that makes it suspect, but is it really so rare?

Like fevers, some hallucinations seem to carry within them the remedy for their own problems. We need more of them, rather than less, and could profit from adult re-creation of another reality most of us once knew and loved, and found very useful, as children.

Two out of three children, in almost every culture so far studied, at some time or another have an "imaginary friend." A playmate or companion of some sort—human, animal, or something quite unique—who helps them deal with the problems of growing up. Some are secret—one in four parents never even hear about the friend at all—but most are so real, so visible, so useful, that they come to play a large role in the life of three-year-olds. Children talk to, listen to, and interact with these entities in every possible way—demanding that others take them seriously, setting places for them at table, drying them after a bath, taking them on outings, securely strapped in with their own seat belts. And sensible parents or teachers play along instead of denying them, ignoring them, or worrying that such visions may be the result of neglect.

There is no evidence that imaginary friends interfere with a child's grasp of reality. On the contrary, they seem to provide companionship when children most need it, someone to talk to when things get confusing during the day or scary after dark. And all studies confirm that children who have such invisible playmates also have positive personality characteristics. They are sociable, creative, and forthcoming, all the things necessary to acquire real friends later.

Few imaginary friends last more than three years. Usually they disappear around the time most children go to school, at the age of about six. They go the way of Santa Claus, the Easter Bunny, and the Tooth Fairy—all distinctly inferior, grown-up, cultural inventions that nobody really misses. Imaginary friends, on the other hand, are ones of fond memory, readily and happily providing security, just when we most need it.

Imaginary friends provide just that in a host of guises. Tigers are good, symbols of power and cunning, but elephants are even better. Ask Lukie. And what if such friends are not altogether imaginary, but have their origin in real life, or traces of it still adhering to particular places?

STRANGELY, there are no elephants in nursery rhymes.

No one knows why, though some suggest Mother Goose knows best. She favored lambs and ladybirds, frogs and mice, but that beak-nosed old biddy is now safely bedded down in Boston's Old Granary Burial Ground, and the truth can be told. . . .

Elephants are everywhere. They are big, but gentle; strong, but kind; very well intentioned and never known to have harmed a human child. And yet, by some curious oversight, they are poorly represented in books written for children.

There is, of course, Babar—an elephant with a well-rounded character. Jean de Brunhoff captured him in formal attire, a

Parisian boulevardier with impeccable manners, a perfect gentleman. He would be welcome anywhere, but only as a clubman, a grown-up with big ears—*not* as a true elephant.

A. A. Milne's Heffalump comes closer to the truth. It is suitably elusive. Christopher Robin claims to have seen it "just lumping along," but is quick to add: "I don't think it saw me." That, however, is enough for Pooh and Piglet, who conceive a Cunning Trap involving a Very Deep Pit. A plan based entirely on the well-known fact that Heffalumps are in the habit of walking along "humming a little song, and looking up at the sky, wondering if it will rain."

Such near invisibility is well founded in natural history. Elephants are extraordinarily good at silent running, standing still, and blending in with the background. And as Rudyard Kipling well knew, they are tidy creatures despite having borrowed noses from a crocodile. His *Just So Stories* are rich in jungle lore, but what in the end makes them so convincing is that the animals in them have no cute personal names. They feature such rugged individualists as the Cat That Walked by Himself, and that reluctant herd member the Elephant's Child, who later became a practicing Lamarckist, passing along an acquired character to its descendants.

These, however, are adult concerns. The real truth about elephants lies in the experience of children themselves, and in the imagination of those few happy grown-up souls whom Dr. Seuss describes as "obsolete children."

Desmond Morris is definitely one of those. While I was working on my doctorate at London Zoo, Granada Television started a series of programs called *Zoo Time* which flouted all conventional wisdom. Not only did the presenter, Desmond himself, work with scene-stealing animals, but he did so *live* on a direct feed straight to air from the zoo!

It was a chaotic, wonderful, anything-can-happen kind of show, and it became immensely popular with children. So popular that it offered the kind of research facility most academics can only dream about. Desmond was quick to seize the opportunity and invented a competition which involved a small prize for the answer to a simple question. But each entry required that any child who took part also had to say which animal he or she liked most, and which was liked least. Loves and hates were the subject of the survey.

The program was inundated with hundreds of thousands of postcards bearing the answers he needed, doing in less than a minute on the air the kind of research that normally requires elaborate questionnaires and years of fieldwork. As his student, I was roped in to help with a flood of paper that threatened to engulf the entire zoo. We counted every card, listed every preference, and analyzed the information by breaking the responses down into groups by age and sex. The information was fascinating. . . .

As predicted, the most popular animals were the ones most like ourselves—chimpanzees and bears, with human characteristics. The least popular, for obvious reasons, were snakes and spiders. This much we expected. There were also a number of quirky geographical and cultural oddities, and a dramatic preference amongst preteen girls for horses, but the most interesting results were developmental. Most boys and girls over nine years old were interested in small, manageable animals, the ones that could be trained or mothered, child substitutes such as hamsters and rabbits. And most children under six were attracted to very large animals, symbolic adults and parent subsitutes. Dinosaurs got a lot of votes, the only dead animals to feature in the survey, but by far and away the heavy favorite amongst all young children was—the elephant!

AS a species, we have a biased awareness of the world. We see not with our eyes, but with our minds. Our experience of reality is both selective and subjective. We not only tune in to restricted bits of it, but also shuffle and sort these out in accordance with our experience and expectation of them. We arrange things into patterns, sifting the limited input and "making sense" of what we do receive. The abitrary nature of this agreement is very clearly revealed by the adjective "consensual": a gathering of the senses, a common response obtained by all those operating under the same cultural constraints. But what we experience and describe in this way, no matter how widely it may be validated, is not necessarily anything like what actually exists out there in the "real" world.

As a rule, children are more open to the true nature of things. Their experience is far more freeform, less constrained, more honest than that of adults, who have learned to construct personal views that are likely to be more socially acceptable. We edit imaginary friends and phantom elephants out of our experience, shaping reality in the interests of consensus. Children are much more likely to perceive things as they are, listening to the true music of life while such innocence lasts, taking elephants as they come.

I have emphasized the role I believe smell, in its entirety, plays in our perception of the world around us, and the way in which subliminal, unconscious odors could work in concert with the other senses. Sound and hearing are filtered out in the same way as sight, pushed through the reducing valves of our agreements about how things should sound and what we can and cannot experience.

Katy Payne has enlarged both our awareness and our imagination by speeding up her tapes of elephant infrasound, and now there is another pioneer of acoustical ecology.

Bernie Kraus in *Into a Wild Sanctuary* has introduced the idea of acoustical niches, showing how different species jostle for acoustic territory or unoccupied frequencies in which to communicate. He records the entire, combined sound that all living organisms produce in a biome, picking up what he calls "a constantly changing, reflexive synthesis of sound." A soundscape which, on analysis, can be found to include even the susurrus of worms burrowing through the ground. And he finds that it is possible to use such records to date a habitat and identify changes taking place as its quality declines. Undisturbed ecologies have extraordinary bioacoustic continuity, a kind of sonic integrity that comes from having every niche properly occupied. In each biome, creatures create audio output complementary to all the other noise producers. And where elephants once thrived, there are now acoustical holes in the habitat.

This is an important idea, and yet one more good reason to look at nature as a whole, to listen to its heartbeat. It helps to understand the alchemy of sound, and why some cultures believe that certain sounds can fill damaging gaps, waking the secret life of forests, reviving dead seeds in barren wastes, taming terrible beasts, transforming raging torrents, and transporting great stones. So Orpheus animates the world with the music of his lyre, David uses his to free Saul from an evil spirit, and plainsong is taken up by Trappist monks to create the lightness necessary for the soul's flight toward truth. And elephants envelop the land with unheard, but not unfelt, infrasound with its subtle rhythms and astonishing patterns. Sounds we have discovered only as we begin to understand what losing them might mean.

Is it coincidence that now, just as elephants hover on the brink of extinction, the Thai Conservation Orchestra, consisting of six elephants, arguably the heaviest band in history, playing sturdy versions of slit drums, hammer gongs, harmonicas, and xylophones, should be in the hit parade?

It is time to remind ourselves that marching bands had their origin in Africa, where they accompanied funeral processions, warding off evil spirits and shepherding the deceased from one world to another. And that the instruments used most often in these rites were trumpets made from solid ivory and still called *olifants*!

I KNOW from my own experience that the Knysna forest has felt very different on the occasion of each of my visits. The mere presence of even one elephant is enough to make me more alert, more conscious of the forest and its soundscape, than I would be if she, the Matriarch, didn't exist, but I do notice a difference. The tremble in the air is no longer so intense. A void has opened up and there is nothing to fill it. A gap where a tooth used to be. . . .

And yet, there is still elephantness about. A feeling that something goes on nevertheless, in secret. There is still a lot we don't know about elephant evolution. Raymond Dart taught me that when I invited him to meet Delilah at the Johannesburg Zoo. Dart was seventy then, a little frail, but still one of the lucky "obsolete children" of life. I showed him the new elephant area and its amenities, explaining how much freedom they would enjoy, and he said: "I feel like Moses looking out over the Promised Land!"

He thoroughly enjoyed meeting Delilah, who took to him immediately. Elephants know the real thing when they meet it. And he was moved to talk about "bones of contention" and the frenzy of the Miocene when proboscids were popping up all over. Later he showed me a peculiar paper that was never published, but did the rounds of comparative anatomy in the early twentieth century.

It was dated 1911 and entitled "A Surprising Datum Event" and subtitled "Evidence of hominid co-existence with a Miocene proboscidean." That, in itself, was an eye-catcher. I knew that the Miocene epoch started about 26 million years ago and ended perhaps five or six million years ago, still far too early for hominids.

I raised my eyebrows and Dart nodded and said: "Even I never had the cheek to push things that far back!"

The next thing I noticed was that it was not attributed to any author, and again Dart nodded. "It came to me with a covering note," he explained. "As far as I can remember, it said the paper was being circulated in this way because no journal would publish it. It was too strange and threatening. It was not signed, but those involved in sending it to me in confidence vouched for its authenticity."

I was intrigued and read it carefully. It was about thirty pages long, dedicated largely to an overview of proboscid evolution as it was understood in 1911, when there were far more families and species recognized. The heart of the paper was set in North Africa, in that part which provided a land bridge for both early hominids and proboscids making their way out of Africa into the wide-open spaces of Asia. And it described the almost complete fossilized skeleton of an adult proboscid. An animal that would have stood nearly ten feet tall at the shoulder and had not two but four tusks. One of those eccentric elephant experiments of the mid-Miocene.

Such finds are not rare in the Sahara, which was once a vast, shallow lake in which many Miocene mammals became embalmed. The discovery of any such relic should have been a cause for celebration, not secrecy. But there was one detail that definitely made this one troublesome.

The four tusks were complete and the teeth were low-crowned and high-cusped like those of all Miocene elephants, but lodged firmly into the left lower jaw, and clearly impacted there before the animal died, was something truly extraordinary. A razor-sharp and beautifully crafted stone spearpoint!

"Uh huh!" said Dart when I got to this page. "In 1911, it would have seemed like heresy to even imagine that a tool-using man in Africa could have been older than the Neanderthal discoveries, which were believed to be twenty thousand years old, not twenty million!

"It was impossible for a spear-throwing hominid and a fossil proboscid with four tusks to coexist! Which left just two possibilities.

Either this prehistoric proboscid survived at least ten million years longer than anyone believed possible, or the hominind who attacked it evolved ten million years earlier than any previous estimate."

I began to understand the dilemma. Either conclusion would be vigorously disputed by the paleontological and anthropological authorities. Nothing good could come out of it, and yet it was a discovery too exciting to ignore. So, it seemed, someone had taken the shrewd way out and chosen anonymity, while still preserving priority in case later finds made the whole thing more palatable. I asked Dart if he knew who it was.

"No," he said, "but I have a sneaking feeling it was that big bloke at the American Museum of Natural History."

HENRY FAIRFIELD OSBORN was big.

A big man with big ideas and a fondness for big animals. His early research produced huge studies on the giant titanotheres and the even larger sauropod dinosaurs. But he is best known for his monumental two-volume publication *Proboscidea: A Monograph of the Discovery, Evolution, Migration and Extinction of the Mastodonts and Elephants of the World.*

His collecting and research programs between 1890 and 1930 made the Museum of Natural History in New York the largest of its kind in the world. And his predilection for bigness extended also into the names he chose for many of the new fossils that crossed his enormous desk in the Department of Vertebrate Palaeontology. *Hesperoloxodon, Metarchidiskodon,* and *Synconolophus* are just some of his adoptees—all well known in the select company of scientists who like to call themselves proboscideanologists.

Osborn was not just a scientist, he was a scion. In addition to his academic work, he was a personal friend of President Theodore

Roosevelt and nephew to the financial giant J. P. Morgan. He was president of the museum's board of trustees, held a chair at Columbia University, and was a founder of the New York Zoological Society. He moved in very influential circles and had everything to lose by getting involved in an unseemly controversy. I believe Dart was right—it could well have been his paper.

In retrospect, it bore all the trademarks. It was a lucid paper, and at several points it used the term "adaptive radiation." Osborn coined this term to describe his belief that primitive forms evolve into several variations by adapting to different ecological niches, but he did not define it fully, or publish it anywhere, until 1921. And he had worked in the Fayum Desert of Egypt in 1907.

The incident of the "surprising datum event" still remains unsolved. There may be an unlabeled box somewhere in the bowels of the museum in New York which will one day provide an answer. It stuck in my mind for several reasons, but what I remember most clearly about it was the elegant and prophetic binomial the author, whoever he was, chose to identify the mysterious animal.

It was described as *Elephantom fugus*—"fugitive phantom elephant"!

I LIKE that a lot. It describes just about everything that has kept me on the same strange trail for half a century. The thought that there may be elephantoms out there, doing impossible things, very, very discreetly.

Think about it. In the Addo and at Knysna, a small group of elephants, not much more than a dozen in either place, is faced with extinction. They are large animals with big brains, well used to close cooperation with one another, skilled in the arts of silence and synchrony, and in dire straits. So what can they do?

My guess, and it is no more than an outrageous guess, is that they play to their strengths. They use their large size to put on a good show of strength, enough to make even Major Pretorius think twice about going into difficult country to root out the last of them.

They use calculated aggression as a fine form of defense. This is already familiar to them, but then they go one step further and treat humans as musth-less opponents, taking on superior force secure in the knowledge that we cannot be sure if they are bluffing or not. And it works—farmers and woodcutters are not prepared to die for their beliefs. They have their own limits and would rather compromise.

In fact, they have a sneaking regard for elephants and don't really want to wipe them out altogether. The last elephant in Burundi was, in the end, protected by herders on the Zairean side of the Rusizi and fed from helicopters of the Burundi army. At the very brink of extinction, Africa reasserted itself, old concerns resurfaced, and the elephant died a natural death.

So the aggressive tactics of the Addo remnants bought them time and an awesome fence. Good fences could well be the foundation of civilization. The farmers stopped sniping and the elephants prospered. As we enter the new millennium, there are now more than three hundred Addo elephants, and they are being accommodated in an area more than twice the size, where they earn their keep in tourist dollars.

In Knysna, aggression wasn't enough. It got Aftand killed. The elephants were on the wrong side of an economic equation; the trees are worth more than any forest herd could attract. So something else had to happen, and as I see it, this herd chose their second line of defense. They used their big brains.

I haven't the faintest idea what that four-tusked fossil in the Sahara was doing out of its epoch, or how it fell foul of hominids bearing spears, but there is an important idea in its alleged existence.

Proboscids are endlessly inventive and surprising. As an order, they have always displayed enormous evolutionary flair, branching out in astonishing directions, trying out outrageous new ideas, and doing so in extraordinarily short periods of time. They present a very good case for punctuated equilibrium, for the possibility that evolution proceeds, not by slow and steady changes, but by leaps and bounds between long periods of leaning on their substantial laurels.

I suggest that some elephants, and Knysna is my test case, may have made such a leap in our time. And that the result could be something new, something worthy of the name *Elephantom*.

CONSIDER, just as a theoretical exercise, what a new kind of elephant—one that might survive even our depredations and excesses—would have to be. . . .

For a start, it would be a good idea to lose the tusks. They are too conspicuous, too tempting to the greedy get-rich-quickly elements in our society. There is good evidence that this trend has already begun. In Uganda and West Africa, where poaching has become epidemic, tusks are a liability. The genes for big ones have been selected out, and there are whole populations with very small tusks or no tusks at all.

Being less obvious and visible would also be helpful. Forest animals are already lighter and smaller than those out on the savanna, and some of their genes still exist in the whole African population. They just have to be expressed again to produce animals with a lower load, smaller ears, and smaller social groups. The Addo herd followed this line, but it would also favor populations in cooler climes where cover is more easily found.

And while we are on the subject of concealment, it would be a great help to avoid leaving such large and conspicuous droppings. This requires better digestion (40 percent is wasteful) and better mastication. Come to think of it, having only six molar teeth in each jaw is very shortsighted. What is needed is more teeth or better dentine, anything to extend the age limit from sixty-five to something closer to the modern human mean. Elephants are being outcompeted!

There is also the matter of security. It would make life a lot easier for everyone if droppings could be concealed. Even cats do that, and elephants are perfectly capable of digging their own holes. They already do so, all over Africa, to find water. It would be useful too to have larger, better-cushioned feet leaving fewer tracks, and where that is impossible, why not cover tracks with a palm-frond broom in emergencies?

It would be excellent too if something could be done about hiding traces of the dead. Tons of flesh and bone is a lot to handle, but there is no shortage of good help from vultures, jackals, hyenas, and all those amazing little beetles. What remains to be done is to organize the final interment more carefully. There has been too much careless talk about elephant graveyards!

And finally, a lot can still be done about better and more secure communication. Infrasound was a great idea and is still going to be very important for keeping smaller, more mobile groups in touch with each other. But there are still channels that aren't being fully used. How about ultrasound? Whales use it. . . .

Seriously, a smaller, leaner, cleaner, tuskless, and more secretive elephant is exactly what is needed. It would definitely live longer. It may already do so.

In 1960, a German professor collected an elephant in Gabon so small he described it as a new species, *Loxodonta pumilio*. He sent it to the Bronx Zoo in New York, where, unfortunately, it grew into a normal forest elephant. In 1923, William Hornaday of the New York Zoological Society collected two tiny elephants in the Congo, which he too identified as "definite pygmy elephants." Arguments about those specimens still continue, but both scientists were responding to persistent reports from central Africa about a second kind of forest elephant, one much smaller and more secretive than the other, but still well known to the local people, who claim that even as adults they are far less than five feet tall.

Ecologist David "Jonah" Western, who tracked these animals down in Gabon and Zaire, believes that the undoubtedly small, undoubtedly secretive deep forest elephants he has seen are just juvenile forest animals, which may not deserve the seperate species name of *Loxodonta cyclotis.* And that the so-called pygmy elephants are nothing more than young males of the forest form in small groups of their own. He suggests that there actually are two distinct races of elephant in the forest, one big and one small, but that the small one is *Loxodonta cyclotis.* The big one is the regular savanna elephant, *Loxodonta africanus* forced by persecution back into the forest, where it may even interbreed with true forest animals.

Maybe so, but there are still reports from the Central African Republic of fully adult animals in breeding groups of elephants in which none of the animals is any taller than the Pygmy people who know the forest elephant very well and give this smaller, leaner, round-eared elephant a different name. They call it the "water elephant," an interesting name considering Alister Hardy's contention that the rapid evolution of all elephants was catalyzed by water.

That, he suggested, accounts for their baggy appearance. "If you could inflate an elephant with an air pump," he told me, "you would get something that looks very like a dugong does today. When elephants lived in the water, all that slack was taken up by thick layers of subcutaneous fat. Now it just looks comical, like a child in its father's clothes!"

I wondered how the apparently aquatic pygmy elephants came to be so small. Water usually allows greater bulk; it takes the weight off your feet. But then I remembered that there once were true dwarf elephants on isolated islands such as Malta, Crete, Sicily, Cyprus, and Sardinia. Elephants there were no larger than Great Dane dogs.

This is a natural part of adaptation. It is known as the "island rule," which recognizes that all mammals in isolated populations have a tendency to be smaller than their mainstream relatives. The Mediterranean species appear to be remnants of a forest species called *Palaeoloxodon antiquus*, which disappeared from North Africa about 170,000 years ago. In the south, Knysna is an isolated island as far as its elephants are concerned, and could be subject to the same rule.

If so, they have had several centuries to refine their body size and shape, and more than enough time to change their behavior. Could there be something like an elephantom in the Knysna forest, derived from and still protected by individuals who have not managed to change enough?

Was the bombast of Aftand and the other big bush bullies all a diversionary tactic to draw attention away from a few new, smaller, smarter, more secretive descendants?

There is room for them both!

ON Saturday, March 6, 1999, a green Bell Jet Ranger helicopter took off from Port Alfred, just east of the Addo. It was being flown by its owner, businessman Ian McFarlane. With him were his wife, Frances, and his eight-five-year-old father, Boyd McFarlane. They filed a flight plan that took them almost due west along the coastal plain. The sky was clear and the forecast was good all the way to their destination at the Wilderness, just thirty miles from Knysna.

They made radio contact at 4:15 p.m. with flight control at George, which was told they were just north of Plettenberg Bay. At 4:30 p.m. they were seen by hikers overhead at Ysternek, still headed west, and minutes later were heard passing over the forest station at Deepwalls. Then they disappeared off the face of the earth. There were some reports of a loud sound near Knysna, but the alarm was raised only when they failed to arrive at the Wilderness by dark.

The following morning, a police helicopter from George made a search around Knysna and a larger Oryx helicopter from the South African Air Force was called in to assist. Nothing was found. The search continued daily for the next week until the McFarlane family, as a last resort, commissioned a third helicopter equipped with an infrared heat-detecting system. For three days this flew transects across every part of the Knysna and Tsitsikamma forests. On the final day the searchers found a curious hot spot in dense forest of the Lelievlei sector and guided foresters to the spot on the ground. The walkers finally made it through difficult terrain, and reported that there was no sign there of the green helicopter or its occupants, but right on the given coordinates they were confronted by an indignant elephant. The Matriarch herself, wondering what all the noise was about!

No trace of the McFarlanes or their helicopter has yet been found. I looked for myself about a year later and gave up in the undergrowth of the Gouna and Rooiels Rivers. Hannibal's army could get lost in those gorges. But two things about the event still interest me.

At the center of the area in which the crash is believed to have taken place stands an "island"—one of those pieces of high ground in the forest, this one named, it is said, after a wood buyer from the bad old days. His name just happens to have been McFarlane.

I also discovered that the infrared hot spot produced by the Matriarch was not the only one the helicopter survey had seen. Around it, on the same slope and right in the undergrowth through which the foresters later made their way, were several other signs of life, too big to be bushbuck or humans, too small to be adult elephants. Just right for smaller, leaner, smarter, more secretive beings!

An
Elepiphany

I GREW up on Aesop and Uncle Remus, gravitating in my teens to James Thurber's *Fables for Our Time*, finding pleasure in the telling, and looking forward to the message that pulls the threads together at the end.

Sometimes it was easy. Aesop did it best, on one occasion in just twenty effortless words: "A jackal sneered at an elephant for never having more than one calf. 'Only one,' she agreed. 'But an elephant!'"

Wonderful, but life isn't always that tidy. We live in an imprecise and ambiguous world. Just about everything we think we know requires a leap of faith, and understanding is very seldom simple and linear.

Fortunately, common sense is coming back, intuitive understandings are no longer so easily dismissed as naive or illusory, and we are beginning to include information transmitted through unofficial channels.

This is one of those.

My experiences are very real to me, but they are novel ones, perceptions for which there is no adequate scientific theory. I make no apology for this. I know that belief has the capacity to shape experience, but I contend that even supernatural experiences, ones that cannot be proven to be true, are not self-evidently false. They have an intrinsic logic that works, and sometimes that alone is worth pursuing.

Where elephants are concerned, almost anything goes. Nothing is too much trouble. I would do anything to sustain an animal that has such a huge and evident capacity for delight. But every time I think I am beginning to understand them, elephants do something astonishing that makes it necessary to go back and start all over again.

Last year it was news from Cornell University that an elephant had passed the self-recognition test by scrubbing a paint spot from her forehead after seeing herself in a mirror. That didn't surprise me—chimps have been doing this since studies of them first began—but this particular elephant took the next giant step toward unquestionable consciousness by commandeering the mirror for herself, keeping other elephants away for days. Thus demonstrating, not just self-awareness, but very human vanity.

We and elephants do have a great deal in common. We share our warm blood, our close society, and the length of our lives. Like us, they are apt to learn, remember, and meditate; and to recognize one another, acknowledging death, experiencing grief, and shedding tears. But they are also completely alien, operating in outlandish dimensions.

This year's surprise comes from Stanford University. And the news is that in addition to infrasonic signals in the air, elephants are also involved in ground traffic. They have a seismic sense, using the tips of their trunks and the broad, flat receivers of their feet to pick up the regular footfalls of other feet, and a pattern of bumps and thuds produced by deliberately tapping their large front toenails against any hard surface. Such vibrations travel, it seems, beyond the audible range of their other rumblings, keeping elephants in touch over distances of more than twenty miles!

What next? I'm afraid to guess, but I do have news.

IN August of the year 2000, after seeing the Matriarch in communion with a whale, I decided to take one last, long look at the now
elephantless forest on the mountain side of the highway through
Knysna.

I got into the forest just before dawn, parked at the Big Tree,
and walked westward on Kom's Road away from Deepwalls. It was a
soft misty morning, one appropriate to my melancholy mood. It hurt
to think of a herd of one; the whole idea is heartbreakingly awful. I
felt guilty about not doing more to change things during my fifty-
year connection with Knysna, but it remains difficult to deal with
authority in South Africa, which has ruled so long by decree that it
has become an ingrained habit.

My mind was torn between this discomforting review and the
sheer pleasure of being in an indigenous forest at dawn. The first
light was filtering through a canopy strung with the rusty lichen
called "old man's beard," the acoustic guard was being changed
from night frogs to day crickets, and my spirits rose with the sun. I
tried to find a trembling in the air, and, failing, I turned instead to
thoughts of elephantoms. If they existed, could I reach them with
my mind? Would they take my call? Do they grant wishes? I settled
for some wishful thinking. . . .

What Knysna needed, I decided, was a second chance. The
Matriarch was probably in her fifties, but not yet past breeding.
There are records of captive elephants becoming pregnant in their
early sixties. So what we needed now was a virile young bull elephant. A flesh-and-blood elephantom representing a new generation. This was the home of the Garden of Eden, wasn't it? It was
time for a new dynasty. This time we would insist on a fence like the
Addo's. The funds could be found to set the coastal forest aside to

allow the elephants to prosper, just as Nick Carter had recommended thirty years before. This time we would do it right. . . .

Then it happened. I rounded the bend at the Loeriebos dip, where Kroos and I forty-five years before had emerged from our encounter with Aftand, and there, right in the center of the gravel road, was a fresh, still-steaming pile of elephant droppings!

I could hardly believe my eyes. The Matriarch was many miles away. I took a very close look at the pile. I turned it over with my toe and it steamed even more luxuriantly. It was real. I broke open a bolus and found that everything in it was finely ground, well digested. Then it dawned on me. This wasn't the work of an old elephant, this had been chewed into a homogenous mass by a good young set of teeth. This was a sign, a symbolic answer to my wish, an epiphany appropriate to the bawdy elephantom sense of humor. A dung heap.

Finally I understood. This was no phantom's work, this was real. There was a second elephant in the forest! I emptied my plastic lunch box and filled it instead with an intact bolus. Then I looked carefully at the road surface and found a few indistinct prints, enough to show that whoever it was had gone north to Jonkersberg. Then I drove off in high spirits back to Cape Town, where I looked at the dung under a microscope, discovered it was all fern frond and grass, and called Dave Reynell, the retired Foresty Department information officer, and the man who had helped Nick Carter with his survey.

"Dave, there's another elephant in the forest. A young one, I would guess in the late twenties!"

"Did you see it?"

"No, but I saw the small tracks this morning, and I have a dung sample if you need it!"

"I'm afraid you're mistaken. We are pretty sure that there is only one elephant left. No one has seen any other traces now for seven years. It must be the Matriarch."

"Well, if you're certain . . ."

I left it at that and flew back to my home in Ireland. Back to my stone cottage on the west coast, to my peat fire and the last of my hoard of vintage Cape wines.

Precisely two weeks later, I got a call from another friend in Knysna. On September 7, 2000, a young forester named Wilfred Oraai saw an elephant in a burned-out area along the Knysna River—and was able to photograph it.

The photo, even in the form of the copy faxed to me, is remarkably good. Between the tall trunks of mature but fire-blackened pines there is another trunk, smaller and more serpentine, busy plucking leaves from the undergrowth beneath an angular forehead that is very characteristic of all male elephants. A young male, around thirty years old, coming into his prime and more or less exactly what I had in mind. Except for the fact that he looked leaner, sleeker, paler, smaller-eared, and more lightly tusked than the usual Knysna elephants. He was everything that forest needed. New blood for a new millennium!

I was elated. This was extraordinary news. But how was it possible for an almost adult elephant to go so long unseen, unheard, untracked, unknown to anyone in this busy forest for more than twenty years? What on earth was going on?

Then it came to me. I smiled, opened my last bottle of fine Merlot, and lifted my glass to the south, the far south well beyond the Fastnet Light.

"Okay," I said out loud. "I don't know how you did that, but it's a very good start. Thank you. Now, I don't like to seem ungrateful, but just in case he and the Matriarch don't get along, how about a couple of nubile young cows?"

I am waiting for the response. . . .

Dedicated, with respect, to

ORIA DOUGLAS-HAMILTON

CYNTHIA MOSS

KATY PAYNE

JOYCE POOLE

DAPHNE SHELDRICK

. . . and all the other Matriarchs.